Indira Gandhi strived for certain ideals during her life time and she gave up her life for those ideals. To pay tributes to her, let us take the pledge that we would strive to maintain the unity and integrity of the country through communal unity, brotherhood and religious tolerance. We will prove that the citizens of India are one and will always remain one. This will be our true tribute to Indira Gandhi.

INDIRA GANDHI

Meena Agrawal

DIAMOND BOOKS

ISBN : 81-288-0901-6

Published by	**: Diamond Pocket Books (P) Ltd.** X-30, Okhla Industrial Area, Phase-II, New Delhi-110020
Phone	: 011-41611861-65, 40712100
Fax	: 011-41611866
E-mail	: sales@dpb.in
Website	: www.dpb.in
Edition	: 2010
Printed by	: G.S. Enterprises

Indira Gandhi

By: Meena Agarwal

FOREWORD

"Human beings consider themselves to be very powerful. The magnificence of the mountains and their high and peaceful peaks enable us to see our activities and ourselves in the right perspective. They enable us to see how small and unimportant we are, and despite our powers of destruction and creation, how helpless we are against the powers of nature. But still, we have something special and that is our invincible spirit. It is on the basis of this invincible spirit that men and women become capable of changing the impossible into the possible." These words of Mrs Indira Gandhi, who was the personification of an invincible and magnificent spirit, open many doors of contemplation and introspection.

Many people in this world try to become great, but most of them are not able to achieve this greatness; while there are some people to whom greatness comes by itself. This statement is completely true for Mrs Indira Gandhi. She was always successful in accomplishing any task that she set out to do. The secret of this success was her determination, untiring effort, and dedication.

Gifted with farsight, imagination, and determination, Indira Gandhi had the unique ability to understand the reality and to take the correct decision based on this understanding. Indira Ji always knew the accurate answers to all questions of national and international importance. The nationalisation of banks, land reforms, nuclear explosions in Pokhran, launching of satellites in space, the 20-point programme are some of Mrs Gandhi's immortal works. In January 1966, after taking over as the Prime Minister of India, Indira Gandhi had said in a broadcast on All India Radio–

'I will follow the policy of peace and friendship with all the countries. I will follow the policy of independent thinking and independent work for our country. The principles of the Indian foreign policy, which are in accordance with the highest traditions of the country and which protect our national interests, will guide me always. I will always remain committed to strengthening the forces of international peace and to increasing international cooperation." During her tenure as a leader, she tried relentlessly to convert this plan into reality.

Indira Gandhi thought that till there was inequality in the world– whether it was in this country or in the other countries–it would be difficult to even think of world peace. Following this philosophy, Indira Gandhi made many plans based on socialism to remove inequality from the country. On an international level, she made the demand for an international economic arrangement so that the industrially undeveloped nations would also get enough resources for development and the economic and political pressure of the developed nations would not cripple them.

Mrs Indira Gandhi always opposed any kind of reservation for women. Her belief was that women did not need reservation based on pity, but instead needed a just and democratic participation in the working of the country. From the living example of her personality, her ideologies, and her work for the common man, Indira Gandhi brought to an end this misconception forever that a woman's destiny was only to be a speechless person caged within the four walls of the house.

A fountain of affection and sympathy used to flow in Indira Ji's heart for the poor people, backward classes, tribals, and the people living in far-flung areas. Her belief was – "Our biggest enemies are poverty and backwardness. Till we are able to defeat these enemies, our country will not become empowered in reality."

She had declared a war against poverty. On 15 August 1966, delivering a speech from the ramparts of the Red Fort, Mrs Gandhi had said – "We are fighting a war on our borders and we are fighting another war, which is equally important, within our country. This war is against poverty and backwardness." To be able to win this fight, she asked the citizens to adopt new ideas and to discard superstitions completely.

On the one hand Indira Gandhi fought with the problems on a political and social level and, on the other hand, she took the country forward on the path of science and technology. The progress that the country made in the areas of science and technology during her rule surprised and amazed the whole world.

Indira Gandhi had realised that technology was a powerful means of bringing about social change. She had said – "There is a very big challenge in front of our scientists today and that is to assure the common people that our science and technology are for them only."

Today, Indira Gandhi is not with us, but her vision and aspirations for the India of the future are with us. Indira Gandhi was the symbol of political maturity. She was a crusader for peace and cooperation. She was a person who was committed for the welfare of the nation. She was the owner of a multifaceted personality. To introduce the young generation of India to the ideology of Indira Gandhi, the former Prime Minister of India, we present a glimpse into her immortal life.

– Meena Agrawal

INDEX

1

INDIRA'S BIRTH

Those were the initial years of the 20th century and the whole world was going through major changes. In such a volatile period, Indira Gandhi was born on 19 November 1917 in Anand Bhavan at Allahabad.

The Nehru family used to stay in Anand Bhavan.

The Nehru family has a unique history of struggle and achievement.

The year was 1857, which was a time of change not only for India but the entire world. In those days, on the banks of a stream in Delhi lived a family, which had come from the valley of Kashmir and had settled there. At that time, the head of the Nehru family was Gangadhar Nehru, who was the '*kotwal*' of Delhi. The Mughal empire, which was on its last legs, controlled Delhi. Another event that took place in 1857 was the first movement for independence. Very quickly, this movement was suppressed and the oppressive activities of the white soldiers started. Gangadhar Nehru did not consider it appropriate to live in Delhi in such an atmosphere and he came and settled in Agra. They had not been long in Agra when one day, suddenly, Gangadhar Nehru died at the young age of 34. Gangadhar had two young sons on whom the burden of running the family befell. About three months after Gangadhar's death, a third son was born in the house whom his widowed mother, Indrani, gave the name, Motilal.

This was the same Motilal with whom the destiny of India was entwined inextricably. His son, Jawaharlal Nehru, and his granddaughter and the protagonist of our book, Indira Gandhi, became the Prime Ministers of India later.

Motilal Nehru was very intelligent from his childhood and very soon he achieved success in life. When he was 36 years old, he came to Allahabad and bought Anand Bhavan and lived there for the rest of his life.

When he came to Anand Bhavan, Jawaharlal Nehru was a tiny infant. Because he was the only child, he was the favourite of the entire household. There was no shortage of money or comforts in their house; the entire family used to live comfortably like landlords. At the age of 16 years, Jawaharlal Nehru took admission in the famous school of England called Harrow.

Jawaharlal Nehru completed his studies with great dedication and returned to India as a barrister. At the time, he had crossed the doors of adolescence and reached adulthood. Motilal Nehru immediately took the decision to get him married. Jawaharlal Nehru was 27 years of age when he got married to a woman named Kamala, who belonged to a cultured family of Delhi.

Exactly 23 months after the marriage, Kamala gave birth to a beautiful girl at Anand Bhavan. The whole house resounded with the sweet cries of the baby. Jawaharlal Nehru was beside himself with joy. On hearing this news, the Nightingale of India, Sarojini Naidu, said to him – "Jawahar! The spirit of a new India has born in your house."

Mrs Taylor was staying in Anand Bhavan in those days. On seeing the newly born baby, she said – "Aha! How beautiful, how delicate, how pure she is, just like a flower!"

Jawaharlal Nehru picked up the child in his arms and said to his wife – "Kamala, see, the child is so beautiful, like 'Indu'. Do you know the meaning of 'Indu'? 'Indu' means the Moon. Our daughter is beautiful like the moon: Indira Priyadarshini."

At that time, nobody knew that the child would one day be known by the name of Indira Gandhi and would influence the whole world with her deeds and would give India stability and would create a new history for it.

2

CHILDHOOD

Grandfather, Motilal Nehru, had special affection for Indira. Whenever he had the time, he would pick Indira up into his lap and play with her. Like Jawahar, he wanted to give Indira a high education. So, when Indira grew up, her parents sent her abroad for studies. When Indira went abroad, Anand Bhavan fell silent. Without Indira, Motilal felt very lonely. He felt as if the '*anand*' had gone out of Anand Bhavan. He used to remember his granddaughter all the time. Whenever he remembered little Indira's sweet and innocent talk, he used to feel a pang in his heart. He had written to Jawaharlal Nehru in this connection – "I am always troubled by Indira's memories. Whenever I remember her innocent talk, I feel very disturbed."

So, Indira's childhood was spent in a very loving atmosphere.

She had the boundless love of her grandfather, grandmother, father, and mother. There was a big lawn in Anand Bhavan. She used to play with her dolls for hours in the lawns of Anand Bhavan and do all kinds of naughty things there. The Nehru family was fully committed to the proper upbringing of Indira Gandhi and to providing her the right amount of care and affection so that in future Indira Gandhi would be able to fulfil all of life's responsibilities fully.

On the one hand whereas Indira was busy in her games and studies, on the other hand she was also surprised to see strange kind of activities in her house. There used to be heated debates on politics in the house, the autocratic ways of the British government were discussed, there used to be talk about the struggle for independence. Many great national leaders used to come and visit the house. Sometimes, the police would make a raid at their house. Once, she saw her grandfather being arrested, and then she also saw her father, mother, and grandmother being arrested in front of her eyes.

She used to think about all this with the mind of a child, but she was not able to understand anything. But the atmosphere that she was growing in soon gave her this much knowledge that very soon she would be able to understand the story behind these activities. This inspired her to take a pledge in her heart that she would also help actively in what was going on in her house. She did not want to remain an uninvolved spectator. But, instead she wanted to take strong and practical steps and help her family and countrymen by working shoulder to shoulder with them.

Indira Gandhi was very young in age, but the activities that took place in her house and outside it left an indelible impression on her mind. Her father, Jawaharlal, had adopted a strict attitude against the British government from the time when he was in England. After completing his education as a barrister when he came to India, under the influence of the leaders of India, especially Gandhiji, he became fully opposed to the foreign rule. In the beginning, Motilal did not like this because he believed in law and order. He wanted his son to become an able barrister like him and lead his life peacefully. But, Jawaharlal did not like all this.

At that time, there were two factions in the Congress Party, the hardliners and the moderates. Motilal Nehru was a supporter of the moderates, whereas Jawaharlal Nehru was impressed with Lokmanya Tilak of the hardliner faction, whose earth-shattering slogan was "Independence is our birthright." The British empire was afraid of Lokmanya Tilak.

This incident relates to the time when under the Rowlatt Act, the foreign rulers had adopted an oppressive policy to suppress all opposition in the country. All the rights of the citizens had been snatched away. Gandhiji raised his voice against this and called a '*satyagrah*' (civil disobedience movement) against this. This showed Jawaharlal Nehru the path to move forward. But Motilal did not think it was appropriate for his son to move far ahead on that path. Motilal invited Gandhiji to come to Anand Bhavan so that he could advise Jawaharlal on doing the right thing at the right time. At that time, Indira was just a little girl. She used to sit in her grandfather's lap and look at Gandhiji's smiling face without blinking. Gandhiji himself had a very affectionate attitude towards little Indira.

This was Gandhiji's first visit to Anand Bhavan. He explained to Jawahar, "Don't drag your father with you against his wishes." After this, Gandhiji came to Anand Bhavan very often and used to infuse new life into the family by his visits. Everyone was very much influenced by his great personality.

Little Indira did not know much about the Rowlatt Act then. She was also not able to understand the advice that Gandhiji had given to Jawaharlal. But, in her later years, these things gave Indira Gandhi's thought processes a new maturity. Rowlatt Act meant the forcible taking away of the citizens' independence; and her father's strong steps meant the strong opposition to such anti-people laws.

It would be wrong to accuse Indira Gandhi of dictatorship – that Indira Gandhi gained such knowledge and such insight from her childhood. It is another matter, however, that the strictness of her rule often made the people feel this way.

However, it so happened that Motilal, who was so worried about his son's hardline approach, was so moved by a cruel incident which took place that he went two steps further than his son in opposing the foreign rule.

Little Indira was watching these important changes with her own eyes.

Gandhiji returned from Anand Bhavan and resumed his political life. There was a lot of opposition to the Rowlatt Act all around.

It was the year 1919. The imprisonments and the oppression were going on in full swing.

Then a plan was made unanimously – that on 30th March,

general strikes, meetings, and processions would be organised in the whole country as a mark of protest. The information about this was sent to all the important leaders. But, afterwards it was felt that insufficient time had been given to everyone to prepare for it, so it would not be possible for everyone to take part in this at the appointed date. Gandhiji fixed the next date as 6th April and gave the directions to all to make the preparations for it.

But from 30th March itself a wave of protest started from every corner of the country. In Delhi, a person going to Jama Masjid was shot dead. In Delhi, a procession was being carried out under the leadership of Swami Shraddhanand. When the Britishers pointed their rifle at him, Swamiji said in a loud voice, "Shoot, I am ready."

When Gandhiji heard about this incident, he set off for Delhi. But, he was imprisoned at Palwal station. When the news of Gandhiji's imprisonment reached Mumbai, a wave of anger swept the whole city. Here, violent incidents were taking place in Amritsar and Lahore as a reaction to Gandhiji's imprisonment. Gandhiji could not go either to Delhi or Punjab.

A riot took place near Gandhiji's Sabarmati Ashram also. Enraged with venglance, the labourers of Ahmedabad murdered a soldier. The whole of Ahmedabad was put under martial law.

The situation in Punjab was very bad.

In Amritsar, two very active politicians, Dr. Safiuddin Kichlu and Dr. Satyapal were imprisoned. These leaders were caught in a very uncivilised manner. The District Magistrate had called these two leaders to his bungalow for talks. But, after a little while, it was heard that the two leaders had been caught and sent to an unknown place. When the angry people reached the house of the Collector, the British soldiers drove them away by firing bullets. Many people were killed on the spot. The whole city was filled with anger and hatred as a result of this.

It was the time of Baisakhi festival. The enthusiasm of the people knew no bounds. All the leaders were under the close watch of the British government. Saddened by the violence,

Gandhiji suspended the agitation. But the leaderless citizens were not ready to bear the atrocities of the foreign rulers at any cost, so they took on the task of carrying forward the movement on their own shoulders.

Suddenly, they got the news that a meeting was being organised in Jallianwala Bagh. On hearing this, everyone set off for Jallianwala Bagh. The entrance to this ground was very narrow and the whole ground was surrounded by high walls. Men, women, children, and old people had gathered in the ground. Suddenly, the cruellest action of the British rule was witnessed. Without giving the people any warning, General Dyer ordered his troops to fire on the citizens who had gathered there. The people began running helter-skelter. But, the bullets of General Dyer were fired faster than they could run. Countless people were killed and countless others injured. Whatever happened at Jallianwala Bagh that day was a death dance of cruelty and beastliness.

Motilal Nehru's heart shuddered on hearing the stories of the inhuman atrocities that were carried out that day. Till now he had been a supporter of the moderate faction of the Congress Party. He believed in the laws of that time. But, after what happened at Jallianwala Bagh, his faith in the judicial system of that time was shattered. He did not want to remain quiet and be a mute spectator to all these events. He immediately set off for Punjab. With him, he also took his son, Jawaharlal. Whatever he saw and heard at Jallianwala Bagh opened his eyes. From that day, both father and son had one and only one goal and one path–freedom of India.

When both of them returned to Anand Bhavan, their hearts were filled with sorrow. A new change could be seen in Anand Bhavan after this incident.

Little Indira was watching these changes very intently.

3

LESSON IN POLITICS

Due to his political preoccupations, Jawaharlal Nehru was not able to pay enough attention to little Indira. But, still a definite plan had been chalked in his mind about Indira. He wanted to make Indira a scholar, a farsighted and an enthusiastic person and he made efforts to accomplish this dream of his. He used to love his daughter very much. All the time, the picture of his daughter used to remain in front of his eyes. But, there was discipline also in this love. Jawaharlal Nehru wanted to raise his daughter with a mixture of love and discipline. He did not have any son. A son was born to him, but he died at birth. So, he used to consider Indira as his son and wanted to mould her according to his dreams. What Jawaharlal Nehru had dreamt of her, Indira accomplished that. She became a scholar, a farsighted and an enthusiastic person. With these three qualities as her foundation stones, Indira carved out such great achievements that her name would be remembered for centuries to come.

Indira was still young when Jawaharlal Nehru was active in the political arena. Most of his time was spent in jails. Indira reacted very strongly to these jail journeys of her father.

Although Jawaharlal had dedicated his entire life to the nation, still he had not forgotten his duty towards his daughter. Wherever possible, he would give Indira some teachings about life. Whenever he was in jail, he would try not to let Indira feel his absence. He used to write educative letters to Indira from the jail so that she would gain knowledge about the high principles of life. These letters written by Jawaharlal Nehru were not mere letters, but treasure trove of education, science, and history. These letters had a unique importance. Indira assimilated the lessons given in these letters into her life. The importance of these letters is still undiminished. These letters are collected in a book called '*Glimpses of World History*'. Besides this, they are also collected separately in a book titled '*Letters from a Father to a Daughter*'. Jawaharlal Nehru had a great love for books. He often use to give Indira books of high quality to read. On Indira's birthday, he used to give her only books as gifts. On the New Year's Eve in 1935, he was in jail in Almora. He sent Indira a book titled '*Science of Living*' with the hope that after reading this, Indira would learn the art of living life in a magnificent way.

That child, who has been given the gift in childhood of witnessing a mature political atmosphere and has been given lessons in her childhood about living a life of farsightedness and determination, can never ever allow any biased feeling to come into her life.

Reading these books had a very good effect on Indira. The letters that her father wrote to her had an even better effect on her. On reading these letters, the pictures of our ancient civilization and the progress of the human beings would come before her eyes. She would feel a sense of pride and respect for the ancient civilisation of her country.

Whenever Jawaharlal Nehru was at home, he would tell Indira the stories of brave and scholarly people. Sometimes, he would tell her the story of Queen of Jhansi and sometimes he would tell her the story of Joan of Arc. The story of Joan of Arc influenced Indira deeply. The story of that brave woman stirred Indira's heart. How brave was that woman who gave up her life by being burnt to death but freed her country from captivity! On hearing the painful but inspiring story of Joan of Arc, little Indira decided then and there, "Papuji! I will become Joan of Arc." Jawaharlal Nehru was very happy on hearing Indira's words and kissed her on her forehead.

Like her father, her mother, Kamala, also paid a lot of attention to the upbringing of her daughter. Kamala used to remain sick since the beginning, but she never shirked from her duties towards her daughter. Although Kamala was weak physically, she was very strong mentally. Indira was very deeply influenced by her mother's personality. Her mother was soft-spoken, cheerful and determined and these qualities of her mother had a lot of influence on Indira. Like her mother, she used to love truth and hate lies and deceit.

Besides her soft-spokenness, simplicity of living, kindness, and sweetness, she also inherited shyness and modesty from her mother.

Her father, Jawahar, was very worried about Indira's studies. But, he was not in favour of giving her an old-fashioned and orthodox education. He was fully aware that the present education system inspired people to remain slaves mentally. The whole education structure was made by the British officers and the British educationists, and it taught the Indian citizens to be loyal to the British government. The influence of the Britishers could be seen clearly on the Indian educational institutions. Nehru did not want to send his daughter to any such school where she would lag behind mentally.

Indira had gone on a tour of Sri Lanka with her 'Papu' (Indira used to call her father 'Papu' lovingly) and her mother. When they returned from the tour, her parents began to worry again about Indira's studies. Here, the political life of Anand Bhavan had become more eventful.

Motilal Nehru had died.

The foreign government had become more cruel.

The struggle was showing the signs of becoming fiercer.

Jawaharlal knew that one day Indira would also have to jump into this struggle, so she should acquire all qualifications for this soon. The biggest requirement for her now was of a regular education. Jawaharlal used to teach his daughter as much as was possible for him. But, his own life was a path strewn with thorns, so it was not possible for him to teach Indira regularly.

After Motilal Nehru's death, every work in Anand Bhavan was carried out with Mahatma Gandhi's advice. Mahatma Gandhi advised Jawaharlal Nehru to send Indira to a school where she would be given nationalistic as well as humanistic education. On his suggestion, Nehru sent his daughter to a school in Poona, which was being run by a patriotic couple. This was a school for girls only.

4

IN SHANTINIKETAN

The duration of the course (curriculum) in Poona was four years, but Indira completed it in three years.

In the meantime, she was growing from adolescence to youth. These are the days of life when all the happiness of life is spread around us. In Indira's life too, youth tiptoed in quietly, and the glow of youth spread on her face. Indira's whole body shone with a sublime beauty. But, Indira was unaware of all this. When she passed out from Poona and reached Anand Bhavan and went to tell her father about this good news, she found out that the government had spoiled all her plans. Her beloved 'Papu' had been imprisoned and her mother was sick.

Indira's studies were still incomplete.

Indira was then sent to Shantiniketan.

To mould Indira according to his aspirations, Nehru Ji sent Indira to Shantiniketan, the school of the great poet, Rabindranath Tagore. Here, Indira would be able to obtain knowledge about Indian culture and traditions. The classes were held in the lap of nature and students would imbibe the lessons of life sitting under mango trees, according to Tagore's education methodology.

"Indira Nehru is coming to Shantiniketan." This news spread like wildfire in Shantiniketan. They had been given very strange information about Indira and her family. An atmosphere of curiosity and wonderment spread in entire Shantiniketan. The students would ask one another, "Do you know who is coming to our school?"

Everyone knew that Indira Nehru was coming, so they would reply, "Yes, we know."

"But, she belongs to a very highly placed family. How will she stay in this hermitage? There are lots of servants in her house. She would not be used to doing anything with her own hands. How will she stay here?" Another one would also express her doubts – "We have come to know that her grandfather used to get his clothes washed from Paris. She herself has studied abroad also. She must be used to living like a '*memsahib*'."

Before Indira came there, the news about the royal life of Anand Bhavan, her education, and her trips abroad had reached there. The students were not able to believe that a girl who had lived a life full of comforts till now would be able to live and study in Shantiniketan.

And one day, when Indira was suddenly seen near the gates of Shantiniketan, nobody was able to believe that this was the same girl who they were waiting for so eagerly.

There were trees of mango and palm all around and on the narrow lane on which the shade of these trees fell, a beautiful girl in a simple dress could be seen walking slowly towards them. No boy or girl was able to recognise her. She could be Indira – nobody even thought of that. Because everyone thought that when Indira would come there, she would definitely come in a car, and her servants would take down her luggage. But, the girl who was walking towards them was holding her luggage in her hands – an old attaché case and bedding. She was wearing a saree of pure khadi.

"Who could this be? Maybe this is Indira Nehru? But? But what? See how much glow she has on her face, how much gentleness, how much culture! Yes, this is certainly Indira Nehru."

"Maybe."

"Maybe what. She was going to come today only. No other new student is going to come today."

In the end, they had to accept that the new student who had come was Indira Nehru. The students were very happy to have Miss Nehru among them.

When Indira came to Shantiniketan, she was not given any special comforts, because Jawaharlal had specifically forbidden the school authorities to give any special treatment to Indira. During her stay in Shantiniketan, Indira learnt about art, culture, and etiquettes. Seeing Indira's lithe and supple body, Gurudev Tagore advised her to learn Manipuri dance. Indira not only learnt this dance, but also showed great interest in art and music.

In Shantiniketan, she used to wake up in the morning, complete all her work herself and then get busy in her studies. She used to remember Allahabad, Anand Bhavan, her grandfather, Papu, mummy, aunt etc. many times. She sometimes used to remember the days she had spent surrounded by lots of comforts, but she did not worry about not having those comforts any longer. She knew that her Papu had sent her to Gurudev Tagore to get education, and she was determined to achieve good education.

In this way, the time passed.

The annual functions were going to be held in Shantiniketan. There was an atmosphere of happiness all around.

Indira was very happy because she had to perform a Manipuri dance that day. She was sitting in the makeup room and waiting impatiently for her chance to come.

Suddenly, someone entered the makeup room and said to her, "Gurudev has called you immediately." She got a little worried at being called suddenly like this.

When she came before Gurudev, she got worried on seeing a telegram in his hands. Gurudev said to her, "Daughter, this telegram is from your Papu. Your mother has become very sick. He has asked you to come to Allahabad immediately."

Indira had to leave midway from the function.

She began to prepare herself physically and mentally for the journey. She knew that now the time had come when she would have to jump into the centre of the battlefield of life.

She was not scared.

Gurudev Rabindranath Tagore was sitting in front of her. He was silent, as if he was meditating. But, his song was resounding in Indira's ears – *Ekla Chalo Re* (Walk alone).

Indira Gandhi left Shantiniketan, took leave from her friends, memorised the teaching about life that Rabindranath Tagore had given and set off for Allahabad.

From now on she had to walk alone in the battlefield of life.

5

SAD DEMISE OF MOTHER, KAMALA

On 20 April 1935, when Indira returned after spending 10 months in Shantiniketan, Rabindranath Tagore wrote a letter to Jawaharlal Nehru with a heavy heart:

"Dear Jawahar,

Our heart is very heavy today because Indira is leaving us and coming to you. Shantiniketan needed her very much. How much she was needed here, I cannot tell you. You have raised her with a lot of love and affection. I praise it wholeheartedly. She was very popular among the students here. I hope that when the situation is amenable, you will send her here again, so that she can complete her studies here."

But, Indira could not return to Shantiniketan. The circumstances were not amenable.

It was the month of May.

Her mother was seriously ill. Her body was reduced to a skeleton. She was suffering from tuberculosis. Indira took her mother to Europe in the month of May so that she could get better treatment there. The circumstances did not permit Jawaharlal Nehru to go with them.

At that time, the situation in the country was extremely volatile. Jawaharlal was in jail most of the time. He was not given the opportunity to look after his sick wife even.

The drama of the Round Table Conference had failed.

Mahatma Gandhi had been imprisoned as soon as he set foot on the Indian soil.

Jawaharlal Nehru was busy in writing his autobiography in the jail and there in Anand Bhavan his wife was on her deathbed. Now, the pomp and dazzle of Anand Bhavan did not exist any longer. When the people who had lived in Anand Bhavan did not remain there any longer, then how could Anand Bhavan remain the joyous place that it once was. When his wife's condition deteriorated, Jawaharlal asked his daughter to return to Allahabad.

Indira left her studies midway and came there.

Indira took her mother with her and set off alone on her journey. Indira served her mother very well. But, her mother's condition continued to deteriorate. It was natural for Indira to get worried. On one hand, her father was in jail and, on the other hand, her mother was on her deathbed. Indira who was all alone was not able to understand what to do. Her mother's condition did not improve. Her father could not cross the high wall that had been made in his path by the colonialists, to be with his wife and daughter.

Then, suddenly Jawaharlal Nehru was released from the jail. The government had come to know that his wife was on her death-bed. Only one month was left for his jail sentence to be over. But, the government released him one month before to give proof of their 'great generosity', so that he would not be denied the chance to meet his sick wife before her death.

In those days, Indira was staying with her mother in the Black Forest town of Germany. After being released from the Garhwal jail, Jawaharlal Nehru straightaway reached there.

Kamala, who was lying on the sick bed, welcomed her husband with a wan smile.

But, in spite of her Papu coming there, her mother's condition did not improve. When her mother's condition began to deteriorate further, her father took her to Switzerland. Here, her mother's condition improved a little bit. Indira took admission in a nearby school there and Papu bought a typewriter and got busy in his literary activities.

But, India needed Jawaharlal.

Mahatma Gandhi kept sending letter after letter to Jawahar, and Rajendra Prasad kept sending request after request.

In the end, he had to leave everything and go back to India.

Indira used to look at all this from afar, but she did not say anything. The country needed her father, then how could she ask him to stay back?

In the end, Kamala died in the year 1936. Indira was shattered on losing her mother. She did not want to continue staying in Switzerland any longer. After her beloved mother's death, she had suddenly become lonely there.

Papu could not see this condition of his daughter. He thought that maybe her attention would be diverted if she got busy in her studies again. So, Nehru Ji got her admitted in Oxford University where she started studying History.

In the year 1939, she was in Britain. The times were changing. She wanted to concentrate on her studies. But, it was impossible for her to remain untouched by outside changes. This was the time when Indira was becoming politically mature.

She had thought that she would not let her studies in Oxford be hampered at any cost. Till now she had not been able to concentrate on her studies properly due to her father's jail journeys and her mother's ill health. This time she had taken the pledge hot to let anything hamper her studies.

But, fate had something else in store.

Hitler's mania was at its highest peak in those days. One day, he attacked Poland. The then Prime Minister of England could see clearly that Hitler's sight was trained on him now. He tried very hard to keep Hitler happy, but all his efforts were in vain. Ditches and trenches were being dug in England so that the people of England could be saved from Hitler's bombings. Along with this, the colonialists started one more propaganda: "Save Democracy from Dictatorship". This was because the sympathy of the people could be gathered.

But Indira knew very well how many atrocities England, which was blowing the trumpet of democracy, was committing on India.

Indira's heart filled with disgust on seeing these double-faced declarations of England.

In the meantime, Indira herself became sick.

Her studies were disturbed once again.

She came back to Switzerland alone again. Lying in the hospital bed, she would remember her Papu always. He would be alone there. Her grandfather had died, her mother was no more, she had two sweet aunts (father's sisters), but both of them were busy. Who would be looking after her Papu in Anand Bhavan?

Indira got well after staying for a few days in Switzerland. She decided to return to her homeland immediately.

Her Papu was in jail in those days.

Indira had decided that she would have to put an end to her wandering life. She would not let her father walk alone on the path of struggle. She would walk alongside him.

How could Indira remain untouched by the tradition of sacrifice that had been going on in the Nehru family since long?

But the problem was how to reach India?

Hitler's war dance was going on all around.

Indira went from Switzerland to France. From there, she went to Portugal and then Spain and then England. She had to cross the Suez Canal to move forward. But the owners of the shipping companies were not sailing the ships due to the fear of Hitler's submarines. If this route had remained open, she would have reached India quickly, but when there was an obstruction in her path, what could be done?

In the end, Indira continued her journey via the Cape of Good Hope. This route was long and was used before the construction of the Suez Canal. There were two more Indian passengers on the ship that she was sailing on. Their names were Feroze Gandhi and Bhupesh Gupta. Feroze had also come to Europe to look after Kamala Nehru. He had been looking after her selflessly for a long time. He had looked after her very well in Allahabad also when she was sick.

After returning to India, Indira went to Anand Bhavan first and from there she went to Calcutta. Her health was still not very good. The famous doctor of Calcutta, Dr. Vidhan Chandra Rai (who later became the Chief Minister of West Bengal), took over the responsibility of looking after Indira Gandhi. After becoming well, Indira went from there to Mussoorie where her aunt used to stay. Her Papu was in a nearby jail in Dehradun.

At about the same time, Indira informed her father and her two aunts about her decision to marry, and that she wanted Feroze Gandhi as her life partner.

In the beginning, her Papu, both her aunts, and her close relatives tried to dissuade Indira from taking such a hurried decision about who her life partner was going to be and advised her to think again about her decision.

But this was a very big quality of Indira that whatever decision she took once, she would never back out from it.

6

MARRIAGE WITH FEROZE GANDHI

Indira Gandhi was born when the struggle for independence was going on in India. In one way, we can say that Indira was born in a revolutionary time. She was the product of a revolution. She proved this fact by her deeds later. She got her education in a very open environment, due to which there was no place in her heart for any religious fanaticism or casteism. This was the reason why she decided to marry Feroze Gandhi without caring for any kind of social restrictions.

A lot of hue and cry was raised in the society regarding Indira's marriage. The self-appointed custodians of law and society opposed it vehemently. They raised many objections to this.

The person who supported Indira the most in this was her father, Jawaharlal Nehru. He put aside all objections and said – "I know Feroze since a long time. He often comes to Anand Bhavan. During Kamala's illness he served her selflessly. So what if he is a Parsi? He is a human being. He is a very able person. He is a graduate from England and the biggest thing is that he is Indu's choice. If Indu wants to spend the rest of her life with him, then nobody should have any objections."

Nehru Ji did not listen to anyone's objections and supported Indira fully in her decision. He decided to get Indira and Feroze married as soon as possible.

Indira was Nehru Ji's only child. He had raised her with a lot of love and affection. He wanted her marriage ceremony to be held with a lot of pomp and splendour. He was waiting very eagerly for that day to arrive when he would get Indira married. Now, when that time had arrived, it was his heartfelt desire that the marriage ceremony should be performed with great pomp and splendour.

But, Mahatma Gandhi had analysed the whole situation deeply. He did not let Nehru Ji have his way. It was his opinion that the marriage should be held in a very simple way. No one from outside should be invited to the marriage. The marriage ceremony should be performed with only a few members of the family present. On 4th March 1942, he wrote a letter to Nehru Ji from Sevagram in which he advised him – "I would advise you not to invite anybody from outside to Indu's marriage. Among the people you know in Allahabad, call only a few people as witnesses. If you want, you can send the information about the marriage to everybody, but write clearly that no one should take the trouble to come to the marriage. They should just send their blessings to the newly wed couple. But, take Indu's opinion before doing all this. It is necessary that Indu should agree to all this. It is her marriage. She can decide to have it performed any way she wants to."

But, Indira Ji accepted the decision made by the elders with bowed head. The marriage ceremonies should be performed as Mahatma Gandhi or her Papuji felt appropriate. She had no objections to it.

The day of 26th March 1942 came, the day on which Indira Ji's new life was going to start. There were a lot of celebrations that day. Anand Bhavan had been quiet for many days, but today it was specially decorated. And why should it not be decorated? After all, today was Jawahar's dear daughter's wedding. Nehru Ji seemed very happy. All fathers are happy on such an occasion. All fathers wait for this happy occasion their whole life.

Indira Ji was dressed up as a bride and brought to the marriage altar. She had worn a simple cotton saree. She was looking very

Former Prime Minister Smt. Indira Gandhi

19th November, 1917–31st October, 1984

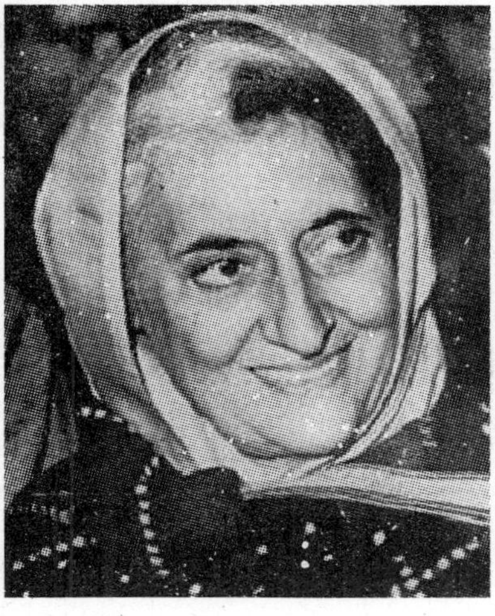

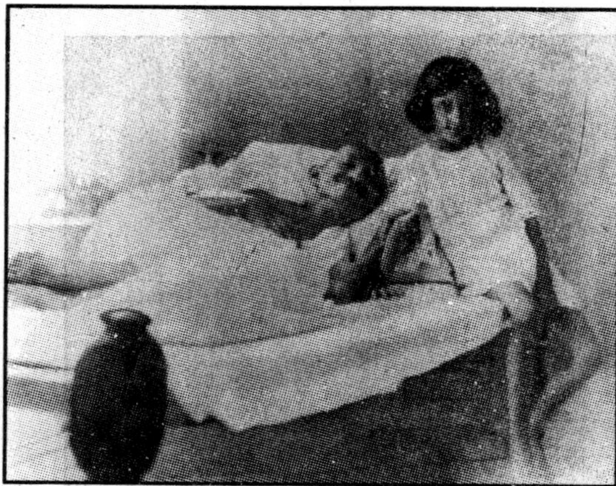

Young Priyadarshini with Father of the Nation Mahatma Gandhi

Young Indira listening to the incantation of national service from Father of the Nation Mahatma Gandhi

Young Indira with father Pt. Jawahrlal Nehru

Young Rajiv with Indiraji

Indira Gandhi with her father Jawaharlal Nehru and son Rajiv

Indira accepting salutations from the public during an election campaign

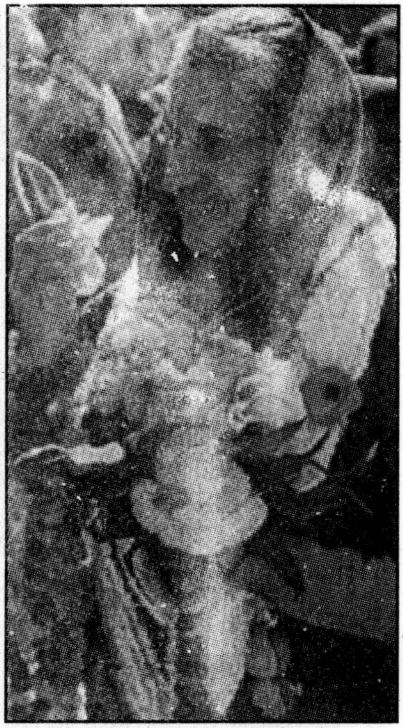

Prime Minister Indira Gandhi with American, Canadian and Mexican heads of state during the American tour

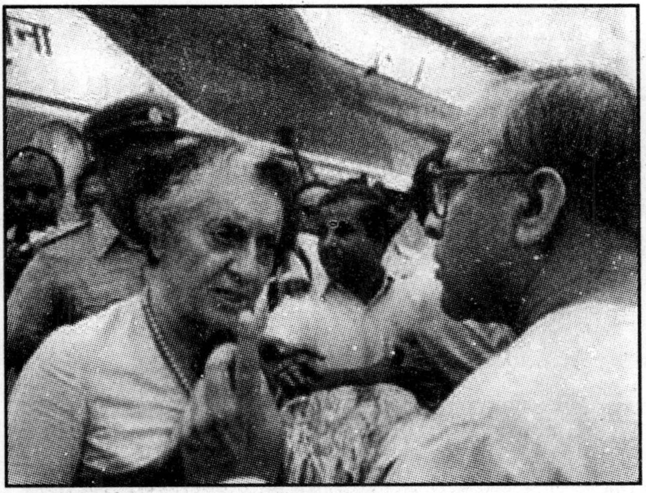

Indira Gandhi talking to former Chief Minister Jyoti Basu

Indira Gandhi with Iraqi rluer Saddam Hussain

Indira Gandhi with melody queen P. Sushila

Indira Gandhi outside the Colonial Williamsberg Palace (1966)

Prime Minister Indira Gandhi with former Pakistan Prime Minister Zulifiqar Ali Bhutto

Indira Gandhi with the administrative staff of St. Paul School, Darjeeling

Prime Minister Indira Gandhi addressing the Non-Aligned Conference (Washington, 1982)

Indira Gandhi in a thoughtful mood

Indira Gandhi with Durai Swami during World Kannada Conference

With Vijaya Mule, representative of cine industry, during Indian cine industry's agitation

Supporters greeting the first woman Prime Minister, Smt. Indira Gandhi

Indira Gandhi with Dr. Seeborg while dedicating the nuclear power centre for public

Son Rajiv, daughter-in-law Sonia and granddaughter Priyanka at the creamation of Indira Gandhi

beautiful in this saree. She was very happy. At last, after all the opposition, she was going to marry the man she wanted to marry. The '*pheras*' took place at night. The marriage ceremony was performed according to the Vedic tradition.

Now, Indira had to leave her father's house and go to her husband's house. Her father bid her farewell with a heavy heart, but happily, as is always the case in situations like this. Papu's emotional heart was filled with sadness and tears came into his eyes.

Indira left her Papu's house 'Anand Bhavan' and went away with her husband. Her husband's house was also in Allahabad in Town Hall. She had to stay there now.

In 1944, Rajiv was born in their house and in 1946, Sanjay was born. After growing up, both of them went to England for higher education in engineering. This was Nehru Ji's wish also. He used to say that in the coming days India would need engineers the most. Both the children joined the engineering course to fulfil their grandfather's wish.

The struggle for independence was at its peak.

Feroze Gandhi himself was an important soldier of the struggle for independence. Now, he had got a wife who was also coloured with the same colours. Both husband and wife decided to work together in the struggle for independence. Only a few months after their marriage their revolutionary activities grew. As a result, very soon both of them had to go to jail.

But, a new and extremist wave was gaining momentum in the national life. By August, the preparations for a new campaign in Mumbai were started. Indira's younger aunt (*bua*), Krishna, lived in Mumbai. Indu and Feroze along with their Papu were staying at her house in Mumbai. Suddenly, one day, the police knocked at their door and arrested Krishna and Jawahar and took them away. There Mahatma Gandhi had also been arrested.

Nobody knew where Jawahar was or where Gandhiji was. The whole nation was worried. The colonialist government declared that because the Indian leaders were indulging in destructive activities, they had been imprisoned.

The whole nation burst with anger. The slogans of "Do or Die" and "Britishers! Leave India" resounded in all the streets and lanes of India. Along with this, the bullets of the Britishers were also being fired.

Indira was very deeply worried at her father's disappearance. Feroze and Indira came back from Mumbai. But, very soon they got separated. Feroze got busy in his underground activities and Indira also jumped into the struggle for independence. One day, it was heard that Indira was going to some meeting to wave the Indian flag there. This was a very difficult thing to do because there was strict police watch there. But despite the police watch, a huge crowd of students started gathering at the meeting place. People gathered there from many places to listen to Indira Ji's speech. When the police came to know of this, they took their rifles and surrounded the whole place. Indira Ji had been speaking for only five minutes when the police gave a warning – "Stop your speech otherwise we will shoot everybody."

But, before the police could fire even a single bullet, someone jumped and caught the rifle that a British soldier was holding and warned him, "Don't you dare!" This was no one else but Feroze Gandhi. He had been missing since the last few days, but when he came to know that the police intended to create some trouble at Indira Ji's meeting, he could not stop himself and reached there straightaway.

The newly-wed couple, which had been separated since the last few days, met again in this commotion and then became separated once again. Both of them were caught and imprisoned in separate cells.

Indira had not fulfilled any of the dreams that she had seen at the time of her wedding when this catastrophe struck. Only six months after their marriage, they were imprisoned in separate cells in the prisons of the colonialists.

But, Indira did not worry about this. She knew that if she

wanted to help her country in the struggle for independence, she would have to make some sacrifice.

Feroze's entire life had been spent amidst struggles and trials and tribulations.

Even after independence had been achieved, Feroze did not remain quiet; he continued to contribute to the development of the country. He became a Member of Parliament. In Parliament, his fearless voice would always apprise the people of the truth. Even today, his fearlessness is praised in the Indian Parliament.

Feroze died on 8 September 1960.

7

IN ACTIVE POLITICS

The year in which Indira Gandhi was born was also the year of the success of the Russian Revolution. A lot of changes were taking place on the political stage of the whole world.

India was also going through a decisive phase in those days because the struggle for independence had decided the path it was going to follow. The successful revolution of Russia had affected Indian politics a lot. India's new generation was looking towards the Russian Revolution with curiosity. It also wanted to adopt the same path and drive away the Britishers from India. But, the whole political movement was in Mahatma Gandhi's hands.

Every big and small member of the family in which Indira Gandhi was born had dedicated their lives to removing the shackles of colonialism.

The truth was that in those days Anand Bhavan was the central point for Indian politics. Leaders like Mahatma Gandhi, Malviya, Lala Lajpatrai, and many Indian and foreign leaders used to come there and have discussions on political situations. So, every pore of Indira's being was immersed in politics. No one should be surprised at the fact that as soon as she became a little mature, she dedicated herself to the independence struggle. Indira Ji has written somewhere in her memoirs that she began to take interest in politics since she was three years old. When the Congress conference was held in Goa in 1921, little Indira also went there and she watched and listened to all the activities that took place there very intently.

When Indira grew up a little, a desire started growing in her heart to contribute to the struggle for independence. She also wanted to serve her country. But the seriousness with which her grandfather, Papu, or Gandhiji were contributing to the Indian politics, seeing that Indira felt herself to be too young to contribute to Indian politics. Though she was young in age, she did not lack in courage. She gathered her little friends from her neighbourhood and constituted the 'Vanar Sena' (Monkey Brigade). All the members of the Vanar Sena were boys and girls of Indira's age. Indira Ji became the leader of this Vanar Sena. Their main work was to serve the wounded members of a procession, give water to thirsty people, take the messages of the leaders from one place to another, and to help in similar ways and to contribute to the struggle for independence. At first look, these tasks may seem to be child's play, but try to imagine that time and think how useful these tasks must have been to the soldiers of the independence struggle. The busy leaders handed over their small tasks to the Vanar Sena with the knowledge that they would be handled very well. Due to these important tasks that it used to perform, the strength of the Vanar Sena at that time grew to be 60,000, which was a big number in itself.

In 1929, Mahatma Gandhi gave a new slogan to India: "Adopt Indian goods and boycott foreign goods". As soon as the people of India heard this slogan, they began to have bonfires of foreign goods in different parts of the country. Anand Bhavan was not untouched by this wave. A bonfire of foreign goods was organised there also. This event had a very strong reaction on little Indira. Her Vanar Sena actively took part in the boycott of foreign goods.

The pledge to achieve 'complete independence' was taken at the banks of the Ravi river on 26 January 1930. Indira Ji's heart was completely dedicated to this pledge. She had said later, "When on 26 January 1930 countless Indians had taken the pledge of 'complete independence' and had pledged to achieve their goal, at that time, I was not away from all this. I also made a small contribution to this pledge."

By the time Indira Ji became 20 years of age, she began to actively participate in politics. Seeing her enthusiasm, dedication, and hard work, the leaders of the Congress Party nominated her as a member of the party's Youth Advisory Committee.

When in 1941 Indira Ji left her studies in England and returned to India, the struggle for independence was at its peak. The Congress was thinking of taking some strong step to make the Britishers leave India. In 1942, the Quit India movement was started. This movement was so strong that the British government got scared and its oppressive activities became even stronger than before. All the big leaders were apprehended. Indira Ji was also apprehended. Feroze Gandhi and Indira Ji were jailed simultaneously for 13 months. They had got married only six months back.

The countrymen had to make the supreme sacrifice for the independence of the country. That country whose sons and daughters do not care about their lives and do not hesitate to sacrifice their lives for the removal of the foreign rule, can anyone keep that country a slave for a long time? In the end, the sacrifices of the martyrs bore fruit, and the country became independent.

Nobody can imagine the celebrations that were held in the country at that time.

The first Prime Minister of independent India was Jawaharlal Nehru. Nehru Ji had made very big contributions in the struggle for independence, so he fully deserved the post of the Prime Minister of India. Indira Ji became her father's helper. Seeing her father's extremely busy schedule, Indira provided him with full assistance in his work. Wherever Nehru Ji used to go, Indira Ji used to go with him. Indira Ji toured almost the whole world and saw the different people and their customs, traditions and different lifestyles with her own eyes. She met the great leaders and premiers of many nations and heard their views.

The advantage of all this was that Indira Ji gained a lot of experience and knowledge.

At first, Indira Ji had thought that she would continue to help her father in this way and not enter active politics. But all the big leaders knew that India needed Indira Ji. Especially, Gobind Vallabh Pant and Lal Bahadur Shastri would always advise her to pay attention to politics. She herself accepted, "Whenever I thought of moving away from politics, Pant Ji and Shastri Ji advised me to continue in politics. Today, the situation I am in is only due to the blessings of these great leaders."

Indira Ji was popular in the Congress Party and in the people outside the Congress Party from the beginning. In 1955, she was elected to the All India Congress Working Committee. Indira Ji got the maximum number of votes amongst all the elected leaders. This was a sign of the fact that she was very popular in the Congress Party. She started the 'Village Contact Programme' in the party so that the problems of the villages could be heard at a national level. She used to do the work of the party with great dedication. Seeing her dedication and enthusiasm the party thought of putting a greater responsibility on her shoulders. In 1956, she was elected as the President of the party. Before this, from the Nehru family, Motilal Nehru had also been elected as the President of the party.

At the time when Indira Ji became the President of the Congress Party, there were a lot of problems in the party. The workers, members and the leaders of the party were dissatisfied. There were signs of a split. On a national level, the country was being divided into parts. Sometimes the demand for Maharashtra would be raised, and sometimes for Gujarat. There was a lot of unrest. Indira Ji was a determined person. She did not get scared due to the situation. She solved all the problems with great farsightedness, ability, and patience. There was a socialist Cabinet at that time in Kerala. Due to Indira Ji's intelligence, peace was established there also.

Seeing her success, she was soon elected as a member of the Congress Party's Central Election Committee and the Parliamentary Board.

In 1962, when the attack by China took place, Indira Ji played a very important role. She went to every corner of the country and encouraged the people to face this calamity unitedly. The whole nation united against the invaders and stood shoulder-to-shoulder with Indira Ji against them. Indira Ji went to the front posts of the army in the border areas and encouraged the jawans. Her work as Chairman of the Citizens' Central Assembly was praised everywhere.

Nehru Ji's demise

Here, Nehru Ji had started falling ill frequently. The nation was worried about the health of its dear leader.

27th May 1964 was the ill-fated day when the nation lost its great leader. Nehru Ji passed away on this day. Indira Ji was shattered. But, she bore this shock with courage and fortitude and once again got busy in her services to the nation.

After Nehru Ji, his able heir, Lal Bahadur Shastri was made the Prime Minister of the nation. Shastri Ji knew that Indira Ji had gained a lot of experience by remaining close to her father. So he wanted to take her in his Cabinet, but Indira Ji wanted to remain outside the Cabinet and serve the nation. But Indira Ji had to bow before Shastri Ji's request and the will of the nation, and she accepted the post of the Minister for Information and Broadcasting.

In 1965, Pakistan attacked India. The whole country came together to face this calamity. Like before, this time also Indira Ji inspired her countrymen to remain united and face this calamity. India not only rose to this occasion, but also emerged victorious in this war and drove away the invaders from the borders.

Then the peace talks started.

Lal Bahadur Shastri went to Tashkent to have peace talks with the Pakistani leaders in Soviet Russia. There he signed the 'Tashkent Treaty'. But unfortunately, the day after signing this treaty, Shastri Ji died of a heart attack. The whole nation grieved for their departed leader.

After Shastri Ji's death, formal elections were held in the Parliament House for the post of the Prime Minister. Indira Gandhi was elected unanimously for this post. She was India's first woman

Prime Minister. After taking over as the Prime Minister, she took the pledge that the progress of India would be her foremost goal.

Years before, on 8 August 1933, Nehru Ji had written to Indira Ji in a letter – "You and your generation are the architects of the future."

When she became the Prime Minister, Indira Ji first of all remembered her father's words. She decided that she would dedicate herself to improving the future of India. But, she was also aware of the fact that she would have to work very hard to achieve this. She remembered the words of her grandfather also. He had said – "There are two types of people in this world. One, who truly work, and the other, who take the credit for the work done by the other people. You should work very hard, because that is the sign of a true human being."

Everyone knows the work that Indira Gandhi did during her complete tenure as the Prime Minister. Undoubtedly, due to her hard work India is in a much stronger position today.

8

AS THE PRIME MINISTER

Indira Gandhi was the Prime Minister of the country.

The internal situation of the country was becoming stronger. Notable progress was being made in the fields of agriculture, industry, and science and technology. Due to the foreign policy, a feeling of brotherhood based on equality was getting stronger amongst all nations.

Here, the possibility of a big upheaval in the Congress Party was growing stronger.

In 1969, a conference of the Congress Party was held in Bangalore. This conference is important historically because in this conference the political situation of the country took a major turn. The fundamental differences between the two factions of the Congress Party, between which a clash of principles used to occur sometimes, came out openly in this conference of the Congress Party. Two groups could be clearly seen in one Congress Party. The leader of one group was Indira Gandhi and the leader of the other group was Morarji Desai.

Indira Gandhi did the nationalisation of all the big banks of the country to give a practical form to the progressive policies of the Congress Party. The kings and emperors were dethroned, urban '*hatbandi*' was implemented, and land was distributed to the landless labourers. To strengthen the economic situation, the Finance Ministry was taken over from the then Finance Minister, Morarji Desai.

Indira Ji got immense love and support of the nation in return for the work that she had done for the nation.

Then the elections of 1971 came.

On one side was Indira Gandhi alone and on the other side were several parties and group of leaders opposing Indira Gandhi. The slogan of the opposition parties was "Remove Indira."

Indira Ji's slogan was "Remove poverty."

The election campaigning became stronger. The opposition parties did not have any specific agenda. In their election manifesto, no attention was paid to the economic programmes. They had made only one issue for the elections and that was – Indira Gandhi.

The people had many reasons to put their faith in Indira Gandhi – Indira Ji wanted to remove poverty. If the leadership of the country were given to her then the people of the country would become prosperous.

In March 1971 the elections were conducted.

When the results of the elections were announced, they were very surprising. The people had expressed their faith in Indira Gandhi by a vast majority and had given the right to her to take her progressive policies farther.

Of the 518 seats in the Lok Sabha, the Indira Congress won about 350 seats. This was a victory for the policies of Indira Gandhi and the great works that were done by her.

After winning the elections, Indira Ji had said, "Now, our work will start afresh. We have removed the obstructions that were in our path. I will try to be true to the faith that the citizens of India have reposed in me."

From that day, Indira Gandhi took up cudgels to end poverty, hunger, illiteracy, and diseases that were the nemeses of the country. She took strong steps very fast and tried to bring happiness and prosperity to the citizens.

But India was a huge country and so were its problems. The more Indira Ji tried to bring prosperity to India, the more she felt that her programmes and policies were not reaching the common people. She had not forgotten the pledge that she had taken to remove poverty. But, she was beginning to realise that it would take time to quench the hunger of this huge India. Yes, she had started the process and the benefits of it were reaching the people also.

But the people were impatient. They wanted the promises, which had been made in 1971, to be fulfilled as soon as possible. Actually, Indira Gandhi had herself raised the expectations and hopes of the people so much that they kept resounding in the minds of the people. The citizens who were bearing their misfortunes quietly since long had come to believe, due to Indira Gandhi's statements, that poverty could be removed if they voted for Indira Gandhi. They had given their votes to Indira Gandhi, but poverty remained as it was before. Actually, it is the helplessness of the citizens that they have to bear everything quietly. So, the clever politicians do not raise the expectations of the people. But Indira Gandhi was a politician who was full of human emotions, so she did not try to fool the people.

Now, the people of India were not happy with this situation and the opposition parties used this anger of the people to their advantage.

Indira Gandhi saw and understood the anger of the people.

It was not in her nature to overlook this anger of the people. She feared that the opposition parties would make this situation more explosive. She immediately took the decision that she would have to take some strong steps, which would benefit the common people. She made many plans.

In the meantime, the Allahabad High Court gave its decision against her election. Her election was declared null and void and along with this a ban was put on her contesting the elections for the next six years.

Indira Gandhi appealed in the Supreme Court against this decision.

But before this, on hearing the decision of the High Court, Indira Gandhi had decided to resign from the post of the Prime Minister. It takes a lot of courage to sacrifice power and position, but it did not take her very long to make this decision.

But, if Indira Gandhi submitted her resignation, then along with her many people who were in power and many people who used this power for their benefit would have become powerless. It is thought that some such people advised Indira Gandhi to remain in power and gave her the example of some technical aspects of the law and told her that she could continue.

Indira Gandhi could not refuse their request. It should be accepted that being a mere human, she was also not able to save herself from the desire for power. And even if she was able to save herself from this desire, then other people rekindled the desire for power in her again.

So that nobody would be able to legally challenge her remaining in power, she took an unprecedented step. On 25 June 1975, she declared an internal emergency in the country.

There was another reason for this also. That was, in 1974-1975, under Jai Prakash Narayan's (J.P.) leadership, a revolution had started in the whole of India. All the political parties gathered around Jai Prakash Narayan to take advantage of his huge popularity. The people had become a little tired of Indira Gandhi's long rule. The opposition parties wanted to take full advantage of this situation. This was the right opportunity for them to remove Indira from power. If they made any mistake this time, then they would lose the opportunity to come to power.

Except the leftist parties, almost all other national parties started the process of arriving at a compromise on the seats. Despite their internal differences, all local and national parties including the leftist parties were in agreement on this issue, that they had to remove Indira from power. So, the failures of the Indira government and the unsuccessful policies of her government were publicised openly. They also started getting some sympathy from the common people.

Jai Prakash Narayan's name had spread like wildfire in the whole nation. His revolution had first started from Patna and soon spread to every corner of the country. It had less effect in the

South, but here also the local political parties had established their influence.

Wherever Jai Prakash Narayan went the people reached in large numbers to listen to him. He was an old and hard working leader. His voice had the crowd pulling ability and he was fully conversant with the techniques of a strong speech. He generated anger in the people against Indira Gandhi, and he also requested the opposition parties to forget their differences and make one united party with one flag so that they could fight against the ruling Congress Party with full strength.

Now, the suspicion started arising in people that Indira Gandhi had encouraged the one-person leadership that was seen in the Congress Party. Big leaders of the Congress and Ministers appeared insignificant compared to Indira Gandhi. Then, the way the Prime Minister's son, Sanjay Gandhi, was being thrust forward intentionally was also not liked by the people. Wherever Sanjay Gandhi went, he was given a royal welcome. The people also did not like it when they saw the big leaders and Ministers running around Sanjay Gandhi.

Also it was not that the people had become completely anti-Indira. The common people still liked Indira, but they had definitely become a little suspicious about her.

Indira Gandhi was not unaware of this changed atmosphere.

Then a historic rally was held under Jai Prakash Narayan's leadership in the Ramlila grounds of Delhi in which many important leaders of the opposition parties took part; and besides this it also had the direct and indirect support of some big leaders of the Congress.

Morarji Desai and his people were already with them. In this rally, the people were encouraged to revolt against the government. Government and non-government employees were given the advice not to obey government orders. Besides this, the army was also given the advice to oppose the government's attitude strongly. In this rally, it was said that Indira Gandhi was hungry after power and was encouraging dictatorship. A large number of people took part in the rally, although the efforts of the government was that least people should take part in the rally. It is said that on that evening, the film *'Bobby'* that was being broadcast before the scheduled time was due to this only. Despite this, people went in huge numbers to listen to Jai Prakash Narayan. The next day, the news of this rally was printed in the newspapers in big headlines.

Indira Gandhi could not tolerate this. She wanted to stop all the activities and wanted to think and do something peacefully, so she announced an internal emergency and put all the opposition leaders in jail.

All the activities suddenly stopped after that. The sound of protestors and the opposition disappeared. General public gatherings were prohibited and newspapers were censored. Many big leaders of the opposition were in jail and many more went underground.

The attacks of the opposition parties grew weaker and Indira Gandhi once again set about gaining the confidence of the people. She made the economic policies stronger and made some programmes due to which the lower strata of the society would benefit directly. Special steps were taken for the progress of the people living below the poverty line.

Sanjay Gandhi's powers grew more during the emergency. Besides Indira Gandhi's official programmes, there was a lot of noise about Sanjay Gandhi's 3-point programme. These points were -- plant trees, don't take dowry, and family planning.

During the emergency, the enthusiasm about the family planning programme was at its peak. All the states were trying to have the maximum number of vasectomies performed in their states, even more than they had been told to. The Congress workers were so excited that they were trapping people in traps like hunters. A strange kind of terror spread in the society. There were a lot of vasectomies being performed – it is difficult to say whether they were due to any pressure or willingly.

People were not sure about the truth of the news being broadcast. Radio and television were government mediums, so their truth was suspect and the newspapers were also giving the same news, which the government wanted. Due to this, the rumour mongering was growing stronger.

We should not hesitate to accept that during this time Indira Ji took many steps for the welfare of the public. But, due to some reason they did not have the desired effect on the common public, which Indira Gandhi wanted. It was apparent that the government had not taken the right step in declaring the emergency. All of Indira Gandhi's moves had the opposite result of what she desired. On seeing the laws like 'MISA' and 'D.I.R.' an unknown fear filled the people's hearts.

People had lost all faith that general elections would ever be held again. The tenure of the government's rule was extended from five years to six years.

When everyone had accepted that general elections had been postponed or that the elections would not be held in the near future, then Indira Gandhi made the surprising announcement of the general elections being held.

Everyone was amazed at this announcement. Within and outside the country, this news was listened to with great curiosity. The blow that had been given to democracy by the emergency was lightened by this announcement. People began to hope that democracy would be re-established. Those people, who suspected that Indira Gandhi was encouraging dictatorship, heaved a sigh of relief. Due to this, at least the accusation that people made against Indira Gandhi, that she wanted to remain in power at any cost, was proved baseless.

It was decided that the general elections would be held in 1977.

On hearing the news of the elections, the people felt happy and surprised also. What had made Indira Gandhi announce the general elections? Indira Gandhi spoke about this herself in an interview–

"Before the emergency, there were many movements being carried on in the country in many places. Holding the elections at that time would have meant social disorder. We did not have much control over the economic policies also. After the emergency, we have strengthened the economic position a good lot and have been able to effectively control the disorder also. A feeling of discipline has come in the people and they have become aware about their duties. In such a situation, there is no reason why the elections should not be held."

Refuting the allegation that had been made against her of using force during the emergency, she said –

"It is wrong to say that any force was used on the people. What type of force did we use on the people? Nobody was able to specify this. Nobody has been able to prove this in the Shah Commission also. As regards the allegation of using force in the cases of vasectomies under the family planning programme, that is also completely baseless. I have asked many people whether any atrocity has been committed against them. But, I have always got a negative reply. Some have accepted openly that they have received money to spread such rumours.

After the announcement of the general elections, all the political prisoners were released and the preparations for the elections started in the whole of India.

Following Jai Prakash Narayan's suggestion, except the leftist parties, many other opposition parties got together under one flag and decided to make one united party. In this way, the Janata Party came into existence in which people of different ideologies and principles sat under one flag. This was an amazing gathering, but everything is possible in politics. Jai Prakash Narayan gave this party his blessings. The leftist parties remained away from this new party, but they made some arrangements about the seats.

Indira Gandhi had not thought that the opposition parties would be successful in creating an atmosphere against her. She was not one to get scared easily. But, still she got some shocks from the senior colleagues of her party. An old leader and the seniormost minister of the government, Jagjivan Ram, broke relations with Indira Gandhi and joined the opposition camp. The opposition leaders welcomed this step of Jagjivan Ram wholeheartedly, but the common people did not like his changing parties at this age and in this manner. Indira Gandhi definitely felt some discomfort due to this, and she became suspicious about the other senior leaders of the party also.

Many of the candidates, whose names were being considered by the ruling Congress Party after the announcement of the general elections, were said to be close to Sanjay Gandhi. The main motive in making them candidates for the election was to clear the path for Sanjay Gandhi to become the next Prime Minister. There was a probability that this time the names of big leaders would be overlooked and new people would be given the ticket. But, as soon as some Congress leaders including Jagjivan Ram joined the opposition parties and the Congress realised that the preparations of the opposition parties were very strong, then overnight the strategy of the Congress Party changed and the names of the Congress candidates also changed. In the end, only those people got tickets who were old and experienced Congress leaders.

Despite all these efforts and calculations, the Congress strategy failed.

The opposition parties explained to the people that such heinons atrocities had been committed against them during the emergency that the people were shocked. Wherever a meeting of the Janata Party was held, the people would reach there in large numbers and would listen to the speeches of the leaders till late at night. In direct contrast to this, the Congress Party rallies would not have so much attendance. Even Indira Gandhi's charisma was not able to create any magic. The last rally of the Congress Party that was held at the Ramlila grounds in connection with the general elections of 1977 also proved to be lacklustre. Many efforts had been made to make it successful. People were brought in buses and trucks from far away places, but all efforts were in vain. There was a lot of disorganisation and chaos in the rally. Nobody was able to hear Indira Gandhi's speech clearly and even before her speech finished, people got up and left the venue.

Actually, the people were also fed up of the long rule of one party and they wanted a change. They wanted to give a chance to some other party – any other party – they did not have any special attachment to any particular party, they only wanted to see the method of functioning and ruling of any other party except the Congress.

The elections were held and the results of the elections came out. The results were those which could not have been imagined by either Indira Gandhi, or the opposition parties, or the general population.

Many big leaders of the Congress Party had lost to the candidates of the Janata Party. Even Indira Gandhi was not able to win from her constituency. She lost from a safe seat like Rae Bareli to a leader like Raj Narain. In all the places, the candidates of Janata Party or their supporters won.

People were sad at Indira Gandhi's defeat. They had wanted to teach Indira Gandhi a lesson, but they had not wanted to defeat her. Maybe they did not feel sad at the defeat of the other leaders of the Congress, but they definitely had sympathy with Indira Gandhi. The reason for the defeat of the Congress Party and Indira Gandhi was not only the anti-incumbency factor, but also that there was no enthusiasm in the supporters of the Congress Party. Many of them had not even moved out of their houses – as if they had already realised that casting their votes would be of no use, the Congress Party was not going to come into power anyway. Analysing the unprecedented results of the elections through the means of a Buddhist tale, Indira Gandhi had said –

"Once Gautam Buddha went to a village. The people of the village welcomed him enthusiastically. To test the people, Gautam Buddha said that all the villagers should put a pot of milk into the dry well at the border of the village in the night. This would benefit the society. The villagers agreed to Gautam Buddha's instructions and went to their houses. At night, nobody went to the well with the pot of milk. Everyone had thought only one thing – the whole village must have gone to pour milk into the well. If only I don't go, it won't make much difference. The result was that the well remained empty."

Indira Gandhi accepted her defeat. This was the verdict of the people, so Indira Gandhi immediately gave in her resignation and cleared the way for the formation of the new government.

The then acting President, Mr. B.D. Jatti, played an important role in the formation of the new government.

The Parliamentary Committee of the Janata Party unanimously elected Morarji Desai as their leader and intimation about this was sent to the acting President.

It did not prove easy for Morarji Desai to constitute his Cabinet. Some people refused to become Ministers.

After a lot of manipulation, the Cabinet was made and the new government assumed power.

The people had high expectations from the new government. They believed that the new government would take some strong steps and bring some speed into the social and economic programmes.

But, nothing like this happened. The administrative work that the Janata Party government did were only to break the governments of the Congress Party in the states and to appoint 'special' people to high posts. Another big effort that the Janata government made was Indira Gandhi's character assassination.

The Janata government constituted the Shah Commission and many other commissions, whose work was to expose the 'mistakes' of Indira Gandhi and to recommend punishment for her. The most important among these commissions was the Shah Commission, where great efforts were made to prove Indira Gandhi guilty of big crimes.

Indira Gandhi did not get scared after being removed from power. Instead, after being removed from power, many aspects of her personality became better than before. She learnt many things from this defeat. She learnt how to distinguish between a friend and an enemy. Her inner strength had not left her yet.

She had the love of the people with her and, despite her losing in the elections, people used to come to her residence in thousands to see her. This love of the people had saved her from breaking up.

And there, slowly the dreams of the people were being shattered. They had handed over their future to the new government with a lot of enthusiasm, but the new government was not doing anything. It was only busy in trying to sully Indira Gandhi's image and do her character assassination.

Then, the internal disputes of the Janata government were also not hidden from anybody. There were some Ministers who after spending long years in the opposition were not able to 'adjust' themselves to being in the ruling party. Their behaviour in the Parliament was as if they were still in the opposition party. There were many contenders for the post of the Prime Minister in the party. There were many factions. Everyone had gathered his supporters together and was busy in trying to fulfil his selfish interests.

The Janata government accomplished one more big task during this time – that was the digging of the *'Kaal Patr'* near Lal Qila. Lakhs of rupees were spent in this whereas there was no need for this work.

Indira Gandhi was out of the Parliament. So, she contested a mid-term election from Chikmangaloor. Virendra Patil stood against her. He had the entire government and all the parties with him for campaigning. But, still Indira Gandhi won in these elections with a vast majority.

When Indira Gandhi returned victorious to the Parliament, the ruling Janata Party was not able to tolerate this. There is no dearth of excuses if the government wants to have its way. So, some accusation was made against Indira Gandhi and she was removed from the membership of the Parliament.

The truth is that the more the Janata Party government tried to sully the image of the former Prime Minister, the deeper it became ingrained in the hearts of the common people. What happened instead was that the magic of the Janata Party government, which had cast its spell on the people, waned very fast. The people were not only angry at the internal disputes and fights of the Janata Party government, but they were also very angry at the atrocities that they were committing on Indira Gandhi and their behaviour towards her. The Janata Party had not taken even a single step for the benefit of the common people. Every step of theirs was prompted by the selfish interests of the factions of the Janata Party, or was prompted by the desire to sully Indira Gandhi's name.

The biggest mistake of the Janata Party was that it put the former Prime Minister behind bars. The common people did not like this at all and the people's sympathies towards Indira Gandhi increased unprecedently.

9

RULE OF THE JANATA PARTY

The rule of the Central Government of the Janata Party lasted barely two or two-and-a-half years and then it died its own death.

The interesting thing is that though the atmosphere against the Janata Party government was very strong, it never had to bear the wrath of the people nor the active opposition of any opposition party, not even the Congress Party. Its internal disputes, fights, and controversies were the cause of its doom. When Morarji Desai gave in his resignation, then Charan Singh formed the new government with the help of the Congress Party. The selfishness to become Prime Minister and obtain power was so strong that Charan Singh did not hesitate to even take the help of that Congress Party which he had opposed so strongly and which he had helped remove from the Centre. After speaking against Indira Gandhi to his heart's content, when the same Charan Singh was forced to take the support of her party, he said – "Indira is my sister."

There is no need to go into the dispute of how many and what type of hardships the country had to bear during emergency. This matter is debatable and is also shrouded in controversy. But during the emergency and then during the rule of the Janata Party, one thing certainly happened – that was that the mask was removed from the faces of many people and the face of selfish politics was exposed. The selfishness of the political leaders became so clearly apparent that the people felt ashamed that they had given their votes to the Janata Party. One benefit of this was the people became more mature politically and they began to realise what was right and what was wrong.

Indira Gandhi had also become more mature and alert. She benefited by the shock that she had got, because she was able to realise now who were her friends and who were her enemies. Senior colleagues like Y.B. Chavan and Brahmanand Reddy left Indira Gandhi during this time of trouble and started working separately.

The result of the Janata Party's coming into power at the Centre was that the foreign policy got disturbed and the economic balance was shaken. The biggest thing was that the morale of the people was shattered.

In the summer of 1978, a foreign writer met Indira Gandhi. In his interview with Indira Gandhi, a lot of light was thrown on emergency, the rule of the Janata Party, and the situation after that.

Presented here are the main excerpts of the interview –

Q: Do you think that the present behaviour of the Janata government towards you is a revenge for the so-called atrocities that were committed against them during the emergency? Do you accept that atrocities had been committed against them during the emergency?

Due to political reasons, many times the ruling party has to adopt a strict approach. If these are called atrocities, then it is not correct. Today, I am not in power. Whatever those people are saying due to their excitement, the result of that will be against them only. It is better if they fight with me with democratic means and with their political skills. Who does not know that before the emergency everything was moving towards a downfall? When I was removed from power, the military strength of India was at its peak, the economic situation was strong, which all the financial organisations of the world had accepted. All the financial organisations had said that the progress of India was incomparable. The people had begun to believe that a developing country could solve its food problem and many other problems itself. We had also accumulated a lot of foreign exchange. We were moving forward in the public sector area. Production was growing and corruption was being uprooted. Everything was moving satisfactorily in all areas. The officials were doing their duties with seriousness. In the first year of the emergency everyone, except the smugglers, had asked with one voice why we did not take these steps before. It is my belief that if we had not acted then, the disputes in the country would have grown. My family and I would have been killed like Sheikh Mujib-ur-Rehman of Bangladesh. Something like this could have happened in some other parts of the country also. The possibility of such a political and economic chaos, which would have been difficult to stop, had grown. I wanted to remain in power because I was not able to understand who else would be capable of handling the situation. I had been able to feel and some of my Chief Ministers had also said that if the Opposition were able to realise that it was possible to gain victory over me, then they would not let any Congressman remain in power. When I tried to show a little friendly behaviour towards them, they took it as a sign of my weakness.

Q: Is it true that before implementing the emergency you did not have any discussions with the Cabinet?

Yes, it is true. I did not have any discussions with the Cabinet, but immediately afterwards, I had obtained the acceptance of the Cabinet. But this was not the first occasion when a decision was taken without discussing with the Cabinet. At the time of presenting the budget, no advice from the Cabinet is taken. In 1966, when the currency was lowered in value, then also the acceptance of the Cabinet was not obtained. It is not necessary for the Prime Minister to keep everything before the Cabinet. We thought it necessary to maintain confidentiality in this case.

Q: What are the possibilities of your coming back into power again? If you come back, then what will be your method of functioning this time?

I do not have any wish to come back into power again. I am worried about what is happening in the country. I want to live a peaceful life. Till when, it is difficult to say. Maybe, I will get bored. But I will have to stay in Delhi because of the cases that are going on against me. Actually the struggle is between *status quo* and change. The process of administration is very narrow and ungenerous. The biggest mistake of my father was that he did not make a change in the administrative procedures. I don't want to blame him because the nation had become weak due to partition and it was a very risky thing to bring about any changes at that time. But the whole infrastructure was one, which encouraged *status quo*.

Q: There is an accusation against you that during the emergency atrocities were committed against the people. How far is this true?

Everyone says that atrocities were committed against them, but nobody has been able to prove this. The Shah Commission has been constituted to probe into these allegations. Some people have brought their complaints to me also. When I ask them if any atrocities had been committed against them, they reply in the negative. When I ask them if any atrocities had been committed against any of their acquaintances, they reply in the negative to this also. Neither has the Shah Commission been able to prove any allegations conclusively nor any individual person. All these are nothing but political manipulations.

Q: If no atrocities had been committed during the emergency and everyone was satisfied, then why did the Congress Party have to face such a big defeat in the elections?

The administration had become scared due to the strong steps that we had taken. The administration was not happy with us before also. In the name of progress, the Planning Commission had implemented a few such programmes with which the farmers were not happy. The workers were not being given bonus. It was being deposited in the bank. The people were unhappy at this also. Then the family planning programme had also angered the people. I believe that the reason we have lost is that we had been in power for many years. The main reason for this was also that propaganda had been carried out against us in every single house. They had limitless money to spend. In the propaganda, they were saying that we had done forcible vasectomies and, after the vasectomies, the men and women had become impotent and infertile. The newspapers of the West were also taking the side of the Janata Party.

Q: Do you believe that interference of the West was also one of the reasons why you lost the elections?

Yes, I believe that the West had definitely interfered, due to which we had to lose. They had contributed to the propaganda.

Q: If you come into power again, what steps will you take so that such atrocities are not committed again?

The truth is that I never wanted the people to be inconvenienced or censorship to be put on the press. There is a great need to keep an eye on the police for this. I had tried to do this before also. Even now, there is a need for fundamental changes in the police training. We will have to take steps from now to prevent emergency being imposed for a second time. My mistake is only that I didn't take strong steps from the beginning due to which the situation kept deteriorating and emergency had to be imposed. But it was also not justifiable to let the situation remain as it was. It was necessary that 'shock treatment' be given. The administration was not functioning properly. The official files were reaching the opposition. The Ministers were being demoralised.

Q: If you believe that your father had made a mistake by not making changes in the administrative structure, then why didn't you change it during your 11-year-long rule? At least you could have done this during the emergency.

I said that my father had made a mistake by not making changes in the administrative structure. But, along with this, I also said that immediately after independence the situation was not such that the risk of making any changes in the administrative structure could be taken. This situation remained so afterwards also. I tried to make changes, but this is not an easy task. It will take time.

Q: The question is that if the administration is not working properly in some specific areas, then whose mistake is it?

It can be considered to be the mistake of various people in various different circumstances. But, basically all this is a mistake of the 'system'.

Q: Then shouldn't such a system be changed?

Yes, it should be changed. But, it is easy to say this and difficult to do it – especially in such a big nation. It is our belief that the educational infrastructure should be changed. Everyone says this. But despite this, this has not been possible till now. Changes can only be made with small steps and a small pace. If suddenly everything is changed on a big scale, then the lives of lakhs of people will become disorganised due to this.

Q: Don't you feel that you took an extreme step in imposing the emergency?

No, what extreme step? You will have to choose what is more important – the lives of a vast majority of people or the lives of a few fortunate people.

Q: Do you think then that the emergency benefited majority of the people?

It certainly did, and the people are beginning to accept this now. We had decreased the prices and we had slowed down the speed of unemployment. We had increased the amount of foreign exchange and, according to the World Bank and the International Monetary Fund, we had made India stronger than it had been at any time in its long history. If we had not left behind such a strong situation, then this government would not have run for more than one month. But, now everything is slipping out of their hands. Allegations are being made against us that we committed atrocities during the emergency, but somebody should come and tell us what these atrocities were. Actually, this happens all the time and is happening this time also. Yes, except family planning because the Janata government has suspended this programme. The things that were called atrocities, they are happening in more numbers now. I am using the word 'atrocities' intentionally because they have given this term to our activities also. I do not know what the meaning of this is. If anybody has suffered due to our activities then we have always asked for forgiveness. But is all this not happening today? The truth is that all this was happening before also, it was happening during the emergency also, and it is happening today also.

Q: Does this mean that the work that was done during the emergency was the normal work? Nothing abnormal happened during that time?

Except the imprisonment of the political leaders and the press censorship, nothing abnormal happened at all.

Q: What will you say about the allegations that the government was being run by Sanjay Gandhi? Some people say that Sanjay Gandhi used to give orders to Ministers. This is Gujral's complaint also.

Gujral Ji used to come to talk to Sanjay in the capacity of a friend. At such occasions, Sanjay used to put his thoughts forward. It was upto Gujral Ji to accept or reject Sanjay's suggestions. Why did Gujral Ji ask for his suggestions at all?

Q: Immediately after this allegation, Mr. Gujral was removed from the Cabinet. It was natural for people to become suspicious that the reason for his removal was Sanjay's criticism.

No, this is wrong. There is no connection between these two events. Gujral Ji was no longer an M.P. – so he could not continue being a Minister. At that time, we were looking desperately for an ambassador for Russia. I had wanted to send Sardar Swaran Singh there, but he had no interest in this. Then we had consultations with Russia also because we wanted to send an ambassador who would be acceptable to them also. Then, the persons whom they used to send as ambassadors to

India were always high-ranking members of the Politburo. So, we sent Gujral there.

Q: When everyone was thinking that the general elections would never be held again, at such a time you surprised everyone by announcing the general elections. Do you think that it would have been wiser to not have held the general elections at that time?

Now everyone says this. At that time also people had said this, but it is my belief that there was no reason to not hold the elections. There was no concern in my mind about losing or winning the election. The only feeling was that we had postponed the election for one year due to a special reason. Now, that reason no longer existed, then how could we postpone the elections further?

Q: Wasn't the decision to not give Jagjivan Ram the party ticket wrong? It is obvious that the party had to suffer a setback due to his going away. Did he leave the party because of not being given a ticket?

Not at all. There was no question of not giving him the ticket. He left the party thinking that he could get an opportunity to become the Prime Minister. He was a Minister in my party, he was a member of the Election Committee, so there was no dispute about the ticket.

Q: How were your relations with him during the emergency? Was everything all right?

Absolutely! He never said a single word against the emergency. He was one of those people who had put a proposal for regulation in the Parliament. It was after the announcement of the elections that he gave his resignation and said that we did not take the right decision in imposing the emergency.

Q: What do you have to say about Sanjay? Is there any possibility of a political role for him in the future?

Basically, he has no interest in politics. The truth is that he would never have even thought about coming into politics, but massive attacks were launched against him and he was criticised heavily, so he had to come into politics to defend himself. He wanted to be elected and come into the Parliament because it was from here only that he could reply to the false accusations that had been made against him.

Q: What problem does he have with the manufacturing of the Maruti car?

The problem is that the government was totally against him. If I wanted to help him, I could have helped him in many ways. But, I didn't think it proper to interfere because it was my belief that he should face himself whatever opposition there was to him.

It is evident from the above conversation that Indira Gandhi's thinking is absolutely clear and there is no deceit or cunningness in it. She didn't have even a little bit of the cunningness that the politicians have.

As has been said before, the government of the Janata Party died its own death and the Charan Singh government was able to remain in power for only a few days. Without going to the Parliament even once, Charan Singh had to hand over the resignation of his government to the President. He gave the recommendation to dissolve the Parliament and hold fresh elections.

At that time, there were many contenders for the post of the Prime Minister and every day people used to reach the Rashtrapati Bhavan with the list of their supporters. After Charan Singh gave in his resignation, once again the contenders for the post of the Prime Minister started running here and there with their calculations and manipulations. In the latter half of 1979, there was not even a single month when hectic political activities were not going on at the Rashtrapati Bhavan.

These efforts by the politicians and the senior leaders were extremely ludicrous. The people used to feel disgusted to see their overpowering desire for power, but these leaders did not feel even a little bit ashamed at their behaviour.

At that time, Neelam Sanjiva Reddy was the President. This was the same Sanjiva Reddy whom the Janata Party had made the President. There was a time when a split had occurred in the Congress Party on the issue of his becoming the President.

This incident relates to the period when the Congress Party was in power and Indira Gandhi had been the Prime Minister for three years. Indira Gandhi's influence on the party, government, and the people started becoming stronger. In those days, there was a group of senior leaders in the party under the leadership of Morarji Desai called the Syndicate. It was Indira Gandhi's courage only that in 1969, she removed Morarji Desai from the post of the Finance Minister when just three days before that she had announced her policy regarding the nationalisation of the banks. Other members of the Syndicate besides Morarji Desai were S.K. Patil and S. Nijalingappa.

On 12th July 1969, this Syndicate proposed the name of Neelam Sanjiva Reddy for the post of President as the Congress Party candidate. The party high command gave the acceptance to this.

Indira Gandhi was not able to function freely at that time due to the interference of the senior leaders. She was especially irritated due to the formation of the group called 'Syndicate' in the Congress Party because they used to criticise the Prime Minister openly. Indira Gandhi wanted to get rid of the Syndicate, and if possible, remove them completely from the Congress Party. But how? When the Syndicate decided to put up Neelam Sanjiva Reddy for the post of the President, Indira Gandhi reacted strongly to this. She felt that if even the President who was elected was a candidate of the Syndicate, then the Rashtrapati Bhavan would come into the hands of the Syndicate and the power of the Prime Minister would lessen. So, she did not openly oppose the candidate of the Congress, but she certainly publicised among her supporters to cast their votes after careful consideration. By then, Indira Gandhi was beginning to become popular and the people wanted to see her in a strong position. The Members of Parliament who supported her knew that Indira Gandhi was not happy with the choice of the official candidate of the Congress

Party for the post of the President, and she did not want votes to be given to him. The opposition had made V.V. Giri their official candidate for the post of the President. Indira Gandhi quietly made it clear to her colleagues that she wanted the votes to be given to V.V. Giri.

This step of Indira Gandhi was extremely risky and unprecedented also: To oppose the official candidate of her own party and that too being the Prime Minister. But, Indira Gandhi was a person who had always taken risks and unprecedented and extraordinary steps – but only in the interest of the people and the nation. So, when the elections for the President's post were held, Indira Gandhi's supporters, who were very much more in number than the supporters of the Syndicate, cast their votes to V.V. Giri. In this way, it happened for the first time that the official candidate of the ruling party lost the elections. And it also happened for the first time that the Members of Parliament of the ruling party gave their votes to the candidate of the opposition party and made him victorious – although V.V. Giri had declared himself to be an independent candidate.

V.V. Giri was elected as the President on 20th August 1969. Some senior leaders of the Congress and the Syndicate did not like this. After about three months, a meeting of the Congress Working Committee was held in New Delhi in which the Syndicate removed Indira Gandhi from the party. The faction, which was supporting Indira Gandhi, accepted her to be their leader and expressed their full faith in her. On 16 November, the members of the Syndicate constituted a new party called 'Congress Collective'. In this way, the Congress Party was divided into two parts.

Morarji Desai had not forgotten that Indira Gandhi had not let Neelam Sanjiva Reddy become the President. So, when the Janata Party came into power and he became the Prime Minister, his old wish to make Neelam Sanjiva Reddy the President became alive again. Now, there was no obstacle in his path. He had a large majority in the Parliament. So, when the elections for the post of the President were held, Neelam Sanjiva Reddy was chosen as the President.

That party, which had elected him as the President, also criticised Neelam Sanjiva Reddy the most. The criticism soon deteriorated to the point of throwing dirt on him. The most vocal amongst his critics was Chandrashekhar who was the head of a national party, which only a few days ago was in power.

Neelam Sanjiva Reddy had accepted Charan Singh's resignation. Charan Singh's advice that the Parliament should be dissolved and fresh elections should be held was accepted.

When the President did this, the ambitions of many people including Jagjivan Ram of becoming the Prime Minister were shattered and many leaders, including Chandrashekhar, made the President a target of their severe criticism. Their complaint was why they were not given a chance to form the government and why was the Parliament dissolved and mid-term elections announced.

Fresh elections were announced.

The political environment had changed completely.

There was no one left to even take the name of the Janata Party, and all the parties had become scattered. It was clear that the majority was with Indira Gandhi.

Dreams of the people about the Janata Party had been shattered. People felt shattered by the betrayal of the Janata Party. Then, they also had sympathy for Indira Gandhi due to the atrocities that had been committed on her, especially her imprisonment.

It was clear on seeing the mood of the people in the public meetings what the result of the election was going to be. Janata Party and its supporting parties tried hard to gather the same amount of support that they had in the previous elections, but they were totally unsuccessful in this.

Mid-term elections were held in 1980 and Indira Gandhi's party came to the Centre with a huge majority.

Indira Gandhi had contested the elections from two constituencies– one was old Rae Bareli constituency and the other was Medak. She won from both these constituencies with a huge majority. Afterwards, she had to vacate one constituency, so she vacated the Rae Bareli constituency.

The Congress (I) Parliamentary Board elected Indira Gandhi as their new leader and requested the President to invite Indira Gandhi to form the government and give her the oath of office and secrecy.

In accordance with the rules, President Neelam Sanjiva Reddy accepted this proposal.

10

INDIRA GANDHI'S LAST TERM

Indira Gandhi became the Prime Minister again on 14th January 1980.

The truth is that this last term was her golden period. In this term, she took a lot of big steps – economic, scientific, technical, and administrative – and was successful in all of them. In this term, she proved to be mature and farsighted. It was difficult to forget the way in which she had been troubled during the rule of the Janata Party. But, still, when power came back into her hands, Indira Gandhi did not do anything with a desire to take revenge. She did not even put pressure on Charan Singh to vacate the house that had been given to him when he was the Prime Minister, in accordance with the rules.

The country's situation had deteriorated a lot during the short rule of the Janata Party. On 26 February 1981, Indira Gandhi presented in the Lok Sabha the full details of the decline that had taken place in the country during the rule of the Janata Party. She said – "When we were removed from power in 1977, the situation in the country was very strong. We had handed over the country to the Janata Party government in a very good condition, but we are getting it back in a torn and tattered condition. Law and order was in a satisfactory condition. Communal controversies had been controlled to a great extent. The production of foodgrain was good and the godowns were filled with foodgrains. The corpus of foreign exchange was also very good. But, sadly, we did not get everything back in the same condition.

Everyone was given the hope that India would progress more. But, the Janata Party government could not even maintain whatever progress we had made, in its short tenure. The truth is that nothing happened during the short tenure of 1977 to 1979, and an atmosphere of indecision and directionlessness prevailed. If this situation had existed for some more time, it is difficult to say what the condition of the country would have been...?"

This proved to be Indira Gandhi's last term as the Prime Minister. General elections had been announced for the next term, which were going to be held in the beginning of 1985 or at the end of 1984. After almost completing her full term as the Prime Minister, Indira Gandhi was assassinated. Otherwise, there are no two opinions about the fact that she would have won the next general elections as well.

This last term was important in many ways and was very eventful also.

On every occasion, she gave proof of her determination and courage.

She did not hesitate to take any strict step for the benefit of the nation. She did not push problems under the carpet. She always tried to solve these problems. She never gave any importance to regional appeasement. She always kept her attention focused on the national level. She used to think about India only.

During this term of Indira Gandhi, along with other problems, the main problem that arose was that of terrorism: Especially in Punjab, Indira Gandhi's worries grew due to the separatist attitude of some wayward people. Besides this, the extent of the regional demands of the local political party, Akali Dal, was so much that it was very difficult to accept these on the national level. Their religious demands had already been accepted.

It was due to terrorism that Indira Gandhi had to sacrifice her life. What type of terrorism was this? How did it come into existence? What did the Akali Dal want? In the end, why did the government take the painful decision of sending the army into the Golden Temple (Amritsar)?

Before going into more detail about all this, we are presenting below Indira Gandhi's interview with a foreign journalist – this interview was not political and many personal questions were asked in this.

In this interview, a new aspect of Indira Gandhi's personality comes to the fore.

She loved nature so much that whenever she got the opportunity, she used to go and sit in the lap of nature. She loved flowers very much, especially those which grew in the mountains during the spring season. She had a lifelong wish to go and settle down in a mountain region where there would be a lot of shady trees. But, this could never happen and she had to remain surrounded by a lot of people. She remained an equal partner in the problems, aspirations, and dreams of the people.

Among the historic people that she liked were Adi Shankaracharya and Leonardo da Vinci.

These are some facts about Indira Gandhi, which French author, Marcel Proust, brought to light. He asked Indira Gandhi some extremely personal questions, which were published along with Indira Gandhi's answers in a newspaper of West Germany on 14 November 1983.

Presented here are those questions and their answers –

Q: What do you consider to be the greatest sadness?

The death of a loved one.

Q: Where would you like to stay?

In the mountains where there are big trees and flowing streams, but only in India.

Q: What do you consider to be your biggest worldly happiness?

Nothing. There is nothing like that. But, I have experienced many moments of internal happiness.

Q: Which mistakes do you forgive immediately?

Which had to be done hesitatingly.

Q: Who is your favourite hero?

It is difficult to select any one person.

Q: Who is your favourite historical personality?

The Indian philosopher saint Adi Shankaracharya (788 – 820) and Leonardo da Vinci.

Q: Who is your favourite real life heroine?

The truth is that I don't think about heroes and heroines. Yes, I am definitely an admirer of those people who are able to emerge victorious over difficult circumstances and spend their lives in the service of other people, like Helen Keller and Douglas Bader (legless lady aeroplane pilot).

Q: Who is your favourite poetess?

I don't think I have any favourite.

Q: Your favourite painter?

There are many of whose art I am an admirer.

Q: Your favourite musician?

Bach and Mozart.

Q: What are those qualities which you like to see in a man?

Responsibility, honesty, a desire to understand others, and a desire to help.

Q: And which qualities of a woman attract you?

The same qualities in a woman also – one who has a desire to help others and who realises her responsibility.

Q: What do you consider the best quality?

The quality of courage in both men and women – that courage which is moral, mental, and physical.

Q: How would you like to spend your moments of leisure?

In studies, and in going to mountains and forests.

Q: Whom would you want to become like?

Like myself.

Q: One big quality of yours?

An understanding of people's problems.

Q: What do you like about your friends?

To meet and laugh together.

Q: What do you consider to be your biggest mistake?

That I leave for others to say.

Q: What type of happiness do you dream of?

Happiness can be felt in real life, not in dreams.

Q: What would give you the biggest sadness?

When India's independence or integrity is harmed.

Q: Which colour do you like the most?

This depends on my mental condition, the season, and the occasion. All colours have their own importance. But, when they are mixed with each other, then I look at the result and then decide whether I like them or not. Sometimes it happens that the colour which we do not like looks good on mixing with other colours However, I like the colours of autumn. I like the golden hue that falling leaves have.

Q: Your favourite flower?

The flowers of the spring season that grow in the mountains.

Q: Which bird do you like the most?

The white-capped Redstart.

Q: Your favourite author?

Authors and poets are like friends. In the works of some, we read and hear new things, which influence us in their own way.

Q: Which lyricist do you like?

Lyricists are also like friends. Their work also gives us strength in its own way.

Q: Your favourite historical hero?

Habba Khatoon, the queen of Kashmir (16th century).

Q: Which names do you like?

Which are according to a person's nature.

Q: What do you dislike the most?

Narrow thinking, narrow-mindedness, hatred, disgust, pretence, vanity, and meanness.

Q: Which is the character in history whom you dislike the most?

Hitler, whose madness and cruelty everyone had seen.

Q: Any military action, which you give a lot of importance to?

The military actions of Ashoka and Akbar are those which I respect a lot. Both of them are famous in history for their great courage and victories. But, the biggest thing in their campaigns was farsightedness, intelligence, and maturity. The result of this was that after the Kalinga victory, Ashoka realised the meaninglessness of his craze for victory and he decided to forsake war forever. Then he spread the message of peace and brotherhood in and outside the country.

Q: Which type of reforms do you like?

Which help those people who are needy.

Q: Which is the natural quality which you want to have?

Melodious voice.

Q: How would you like to die?

With glory and respect. I would like to die such a death by which those who love me would feel the least amount of pain.

Q: Your present mental situation?

One of sadness at the present situation in the world.

Q: Your motto?

Nothing.

It is clear from this interview that Indira Gandhi was a generous, large-hearted, sensitive, and emotional person. Besides this, she was also determined, stable, and of powerful and solid intentions. If her working style is analysed in the context of this interview, then we realise that after taking tough decisions, she would go through a lot of pain and mental turmoil. But, for national good, she always shook away that emotional side and gave importance to her duty. She never gave any thought to personal problems.

11

SANJAY'S PREMATURE DEATH

Indira Gandhi's last term was undoubtedly one in which she had many achievements. But, her last term was also one in which there were many sad incidents, one of which was her own assassination.

But, the biggest sad incident in this term of hers was the death of her younger son, Sanjay.

Only five months after her coming into power, on 23 June 1980, Sanjay Gandhi was killed early in the morning in an aeroplane crash in New Delhi.

At that time, Sanjay Gandhi was at the peak of his professional life. At the age of only 34 years, he had achieved many big successes in the political arena. In the mid-term elections of 1980, he was elected from Amethi as a Member of Parliament. He held the important position of General Secretary in the Congress (I) Party.

There was a very strong possibility of him becoming the next Prime Minister of India after Indira Gandhi.

But, on 23rd June, this possibility also died forever along with Sanjay Gandhi. His eventful life ended in an aeroplane accident.

It was not easy for Indira Gandhi to bear this heartbreaking blow. She was a mother and her young son had died an untimely death. But, everyone saw her trying to bear this calamity with composure. The high position that she was in did not allow her to even cry in peace and come to terms with the tragedy that had befallen her. Then, she was not only the mother of a son, but she was also a mother to the thousands of Indian people. She was an equal partner in their troubles and tribulations. What importance did her personal sorrow have in front of that! Although she had been dealt a very big blow, she did not let anyone see her sorrow. She put black spectacles on her eyes so that nobody could see the tears brimming in her eyes.

Sanjay Gandhi had risen like a storm in Indian politics; although initially he did not have any interest in politics. He was more inclined towards technology. His initial education was at St. Columba's School of Delhi. After passing the Senior Cambridge examination in 1965, he decided to get full time technical training. He had developed an interest in the manufacturing of cars – he wanted to obtain full knowledge about this field. So, he was sent to London where he obtained practical knowledge of car manufacturing in the factory of the Rolls Royce Company. When he returned to Delhi after completing his training there, the idea of making a small car had gripped him very firmly. In the beginning, he tried to turn his plan of making a small car into reality in a motor garage in Old Delhi. When he got some success in this, his hopes went up. He wanted to bring a low-priced small car into the market. For this, he asked permission from the government. In 1968, the government gave him the permission to manufacture a small car. Now, all the obstacles had been removed from his path. The complete planning for Maruti was done. When the need for land for the factory arose, the Haryana government gave him land in Gurgaon. All this happened very quickly and we have to accept that, due to his being the son of the Prime Minister, all the facilities were given to him very quickly. All this was done to flatter the Prime Minister also. Indira Gandhi faced a danger not only from the attacks of the opposition, but also from the flatterers in her own party. It should also be accepted that Sanjay Gandhi was talented, because one cannot become successful solely due to being the son of the Prime Minister. The ambition to be successful is also required for this. Only then can advantage of being the Prime Minister's son be taken, which Sanjay Gandhi took. He married Maneka on 30th September 1974. In the general elections of 1977, he was a candidate of the Congress Party from Amethi. But, in these elections, many big leaders including Indira Gandhi lost, so Sanjay Gandhi also suffered the same fate.

From 1977 to 1979, Sanjay Gandhi was in the clutches of many enquiry commissions that had been set up by the Janata Party government. He spent these years in great mental distress. After this came the mid-term elections of 1980 in which he won from Amethi.

He had as much interest in flying planes as he had in making cars. Whenever he got the opportunity, he would go to Safdarjung Airport in New Delhi and used to do aerobatics with his plane.

At that time, a new aerobatic plane called Pitts S2A had come to the airport. Sanjay Gandhi had returned only one day before from a function in Ladakh, which he had attended along with his mother and wife. He used to stay with his mother at Safdarjung Road, despite the fact that he had got a bungalow at Willingdon Crescent due to being a Member of Parliament. The next day, on 23 June, he took his favourite Matador car and reached Safdarjung Airport. He wanted to fly the Pitts S2A aeroplane. He took off on the flight with Captain Saxena and went high into the sky and started taking somersaults in the air. This was his last flight. He, along with Captain Saxena, was killed in the crash of this plane.

Indira Gandhi bore this horrifying and shocking calamity with remarkable courage and fortitude and immersed herself in carrying out her duties towards the nation.

The years ahead were years of progress – the years of Indira Gandhi's success.

In the year 1982, with her inspiration, the Asian Games were held in India in New Delhi. During the rule of the Janata government, it seemed doubtful that these games would be held. In 1962, this competition of the Asian countries had become possible due to the blessings of the then Prime Minister, Jawaharlal Nehru. By organising these games exactly 20 years after that in India, Indira Gandhi had given new glory to the nation. Undoubtedly, India's prestige in the world of sports grew internationally and a new interest in sports was awakened in the country.

The next year, in 1983, one more international event was organised in New Delhi. This was the seventh conference of the Non-Aligned Nations. Who doesn't know that India played an important role in the starting of the Non-Aligned Movement? India was at the forefront of the nations who played an important part in starting the Non-Aligned Movement. Many member countries of Africa and many third world nations reached New Delhi to take part in this conference. A grand function was held in Vigyan Bhavan in New Delhi to mark the start of the conference. In this function, the President of Cuba, Fidel Castro, on the completion of his term as Chairman of the Non-Aligned Movement, announced Indira Gandhi to be the next Chairperson of the movement, with the approval of everyone present. Due to this conference, India's prestige grew internationally, and in the political circles its opinion was given more weight than before.

India's foreign policy has its own importance and, in these years, many important aspects of India's foreign policy came to the front. Friendly ties with all nations, especially with the neighbouring nations, has been an integral part of India's foreign policy.

If India had been able to become a vocal spokesman for the poor and third world nations, then it was only due to Indira Gandhi. Whenever she got the opportunity, she spoke on behalf of these nations in the international fora. India's campaign against colonialism, imperialism, and racism is world famous. India had always given its support to the fight for independence of the exploited and enslaved African nations. If Indira Gandhi had been able to do this, then it was only due to the fact that India's mentality was like this. It is true that India had herself been enslaved and had suffered due to colonialism. All this had happened before Indira Gandhi's eyes. But, she had not turned India's foreign policy in this direction because of this only, and also not only because she was the daughter of Pandit Jawaharlal Nehru who had encouraged these policies. Definitely, there must have been some effect of these facts, but an even bigger effect than these was India's ancient philosophy whose ideal principle is *'Vasudhaiva Kutumbakam'* meaning 'The whole world is one family'. To formulate the domestic policies also the help of these ancient Indian traditions was taken. She wanted to create an India based on the principles of religious tolerance and equality.

She wanted to see India self-sufficient and happy. She worked for the development of small cottage industries and also of very big industries, for complete all-sided development of India. She gave loans to the small artisans, farmers, and businessmen through nationalised banks. The result of this is that today small industries are established in many houses of India, and India is completely self-sufficient.

How fast the progress in the technical areas has been can be gauged from the fact that electricity has reached every single village of India. Modern electronic gadgets such as television, computer, and mobile phone have reached far-flung areas also.

India's first space traveller, Squadron Leader Rakesh Sharma, had gone to space with his Russian fellow travellers in the middle of 1984.

These are some of the big and small achievements of Indira Gandhi's last term as Prime Minister.

But, there were problems also. As long as we exist, there will be problems also. But, there are some problems, which become very complex due to some reasons.

One such problem was the Punjab problem. Its complexity can be gauged from the fact that due to this problem, Indira Gandhi had to sacrifice her life.

12

PUNJAB PROBLEM

The Punjab problem was very old. It dated back to the time when India got its independence. But, before this, it was not so complex and neither did it include terrorism.

We will not go into the details of the Punjab problem. But, we will only say that the Akali Dal had some demands, which it wanted the Central Government to accept. In this context, we would like to say that because the Akali Dal was a political party, its demands kept changing and increasing with time.

The problem is that when a political party is regional and when it has a connection with a particular community, then every issue becomes more sensitive, delicate, and complex. Then, if religion is also added to such a party, then the danger increases even more.

Akali Dal is not a representative party of all the Sikhs of Punjab, but it has influence in Punjab, especially due to having right over the gurudwaras. The demands of the party at that time were many–political, administrative, religious, and constitutional.

In the national interest, many of their demands were accepted. Most of the religious demands had been accepted before. Discussions were going on about those demands due to which other states were going to be affected. One of their new demands, which had arisen in the beginning of 1984, was that in a line of the Constitution the Sikhs had been kept in the same category as the Hindus. Their demand was that the Sikhs should be given a separate identity.

Although there is nothing in that line of the Constitution due to which the need to change that line would be felt, the question is why was this demand raised that Hindus and Sikhs should be put separately. From the historical perspective, this seems to be even more inappropriate. After all, will the Hindus and Sikhs become separate on someone's saying so? Do blood ties ever have separate religions? Till some years ago, no one knew that Sikhs and Hindus were separate religions. When, in one family, one brother is Sikh and the other is Hindu, then how can these be two different religions? The customs of both religions are also very similar. The Sikhs believe in the Hindu gods and goddesses and the Hindus believe in the Sikh Gurus. Both have the same culture and the same way of living. The difference between the two is only as much as between two sects of the Hindu religion.

History will never forgive those people who were creating differences between the Hindus and Sikhs to fulfil their political selfishness. Even otherwise, the attempt to divide human beings on any basis is reprehensible.

Indira Gandhi did not like politics based on hatred, separatism, or division at all; and due to this reason, she was saddened by the developments in Punjab.

But, still the demands of the Akali Dal were there, which were provoking the feelings of the Sikhs.

Some Sikh leaders who used to stay abroad and who did not have any interest in India and had become puppets in the hands of some foreign powers were provoking the separatist feelings of some Sikhs. These people gathered around Sant Bhindrawale and started demanding a separate state 'Khalistan' for Sikhs. These were only a handful of people, but still they were armed with the latest weapons. They adopted the path of terrorism and spread chaos in the normal life of Punjab. Both the Hindus and Sikhs were terror-stricken by their cruel activities.

The movement went out of the hands of the Akali Dal, which till now had the reins of the movement in its hands, and it shipped into the hands of the terrorists. The Akali Dal didn't know what to do and the activities of the terrorists were going on in full swing.

Every day, there used to be incidents of looting, arson, murder, and kidnapping in Punjab. All these acts were carried out by terrorists. It is said that some people used to come fully armed out of the Golden Temple, carry out their terrorist activities and return to the Golden Temple. Golden Temple was the permanent residence of Sant Bhindrawale. The elected leaders of the Akali Dal, Longowal and Tohra, did not have any control over what was going on in the Golden Temple. The Golden Temple was under the administration of the Akali Dal, but it no longer had any control over the unlawful activities that were carried out from there. The government told the Akali Dal many times to sex free the Golden Temple from the terrorists. The news was coming out that ammunition and weapons were being collected there in abundance.

The terrorists were making the demand for Khalistan. The map they had made of Khalistan included the full area of Punjab, and also some parts of Rajasthan, Delhi, Jammu, and Haryana. The surprising thing is that it did not mention Lahore anywhere. Lahore was a big centre of '*Punjabiyat*' in the days of the United Punjab. They never raised the demand for parts of United Punjab which were in Pakistan. In Pakistan, Guru Nanak Dev's holy birth place, Talwandi, is there which is now called Nankana Sahab. None of the Sikh leaders who lived abroad and supported Khalistan and those in India, who took the help of terrorism to make the demand for Khalistan, ever thought of assimilating Nankana Sahab in Khalistan. Even if they did not want it to be assimilated with Khalistan, they could at least have asked Pakistan to give it a status like Vatican City.

Here, we want to make it clear that the majority of the Sikh population of India was totally against Khalistan. Akali Dal never made any such separatist demand, but it also did not try to silence those misguided people who were making this demand.

The need was to look at the Punjab problem in the right

perspective, to understand the problem fully. Indira Gandhi's heart and mind were also pained by this problem.

What did Indira Ji think about all these problems? Was this truly a problem and what were Indira Gandhi's thoughts about solving this problem? In the beginning of 1984, the editor of '*Saptahik Hindustan*', Sheela Jhunjhunwala, took an interview of the Prime Minister. On this occasion, she had a long talk with Indira Gandhi, which we are presenting here. We can understand the problem more easily through this conversation. Sheela Jhunjhunwala had written–

"All the peace-loving citizens of India have been shaken up by the violence and the growing terrorism that has been going on in Punjab for a long time. Whatever is coming to the front is only this that the lives of the innocent citizens of Punjab are being played with. Most of the people killed during the violent activities were innocent and helpless, who did not have any attachment to politics nor anything to do with it. These were those people who were busy in the struggle of life with peace and happiness. There is no dearth of such incidents when a person walking on the road was shot dead without any reason, without any enmity; or a person who was going for his work or a passenger who was going in a bus was killed. Such incidents happened afterwards in Haryana also. The anti-social elements, who either do not want to see the country prosper or want to fulfil their political selfishness by such incidents, are having a field day in this atmosphere filled with fear and suspicion. One very dangerous and worrisome thing that has come forward in the last two or three months is the crack that has come into our national unity. No country can bear a crack of this type in its unity. It definitely becomes a cause of worry for all peace-loving citizens of the country.

When I met Mrs. Indira Gandhi for an informal interview in her room in the Parliament, I felt that there was a lot of worry in her heart and mind about the violence that was going on in the country. This worry was not only that of a Prime Minister, but also that of a mother, a sister, and a daughter.

One of the first questions that arose during the conversation was that after all who were those people who were killing others so ruthlessly? Akali Sikhs and Hindus both were an integral part of this country. It cannot even be imagined that without either of them the structure of the country would be complete. The Akali Sikhs also know this fact very well and so do the Hindus. Despite this, continuous efforts were being made to divide these two. Looting, killing of innocent citizens, crimes, and conspiracies were being carried out full-scale. Then, the question arises: after all what are those situations due to which this was happening? Who are those people who are doing this, who neither belong fully to the Sikh religion nor to the Hindu religion? What are those reasons due to which the people who are trying to put a crack in India's unity, those masked faces, are getting this opportunity to create an atmosphere of violence in the country?

It is very important for the nation to find answers to these worrisome problems. The answers to these problems cannot be found by provocative and irresponsible statements. These questions are no longer the questions of the demands of any state or community, but have become questions of national unity. It is possible to think about these only when the small personal selfishness and the attitude to take advantage of situations for petty party politics are discarded. Today, every intelligent citizen of the country is worried about the problems of Punjab and Haryana. The Prime Minister is also worried. The protestors know that the solution to the problem cannot be found by raising slogans, bandhs, strikes, or processions, but at the table through talks. Every problem can be solved by faith and by talks. Many attempts were made to come together at the table and talk about these problems. In the tripartite meeting held a few days back in Delhi, the government, Akali Dal leaders, and the leaders of the opposition were present. Before any results could be arrived at, due to lack of interest and suspicion, the talks broke down. Suddenly, the announcement was made by the Akali leadership that the Akalis would not take part in the tripartite meeting now. After that, the incident of the Akali

Dal burning Article 25 of the Constitution took place. Whatever happened in Haryana was also not very encouraging. The people should not have taken the law into their own hands.

The problem, which looked as if it was going to be solved, became more complicated and a peaceful solution to the problem could not be found. What is her next step? On being asked this, Mrs. Gandhi said that she was ready to meet the Akali leaders, but how could any talk be held in an atmosphere of violence? The first step should be to stop the violence. The atmosphere of hatred that had spread all around should be removed. If we truly want to find the solution to the problem, then the feeling of bitterness and enmity should be removed immediately. When I say this thing then I mean that I do not believe in threatening. If the atmosphere for the talks is created, the killing of innocent people and the continuous terrorist activities are stopped, then I am ready to talk. I have never refused to talk. I am even ready to go to Punjab. If it is of any benefit, then I am ready to meet the sants also, but on a human basis, not at the point of a rifle's muzzle.

Mrs. Indira Gandhi's statements were absolutely correct. No talks could be held in the present atmosphere full of terror. Along with the rest of the citizens, the Sikh community had also not supported the burning of Article 25 of the Constitution. Conversations with many Sikh intellectuals reveal that they thought that this act was not only wrong, misguided, against the law, but also sad and it would have the wrong effect on other parts of the country as well.

The Prime Minister had this to say about the situation and the atmosphere in Punjab, "No particular community can be held responsible for this." According to her, the foundations for the violence in Punjab were laid by the Akali movement and now the movement had gone out of the hands of the Akali leadership. She cited many reasons for this fierce lawlessness. Most important of these were – selfishness of the political parties, communalism, anti-social elements, and personal enmity in many cases. When the question about the administration and law was raised, she said that legal action was being taken, but the atmosphere of fear had become so widespread that no one was willing to come in front and give evidence against the criminals.

Mrs. Indira Gandhi narrated an experience of hers by which the strangeness of this atmosphere of fear becomes fully evident. She said that recently a judge, who was a supporter of Congress (I), had come to meet her. He said, "The atmosphere of fear has become so strong that people are not giving evidence against the criminals. Due to lack of evidence, appropriate punishment cannot be given to the criminals. They have to be acquitted and they resume their violent activities."

One question that is arising again and again in the nation is: did the cycle of violence that started in Punjab happen because immediate decision was not taken on the demands of the Akalis and they have been shown more leniency? When I raised this question, the Prime Minister said – "This is not the issue of Punjab only, other states are also connected with it. We can't agree to every demand of theirs. The situation can either be solved by talks or by a tribunal. I have already put forward a proposal regarding this, but till now I don't have full faith that the Akalis will accept the decision of the tribunal. The talks always come to a point and then break down. They always backtrack and raise new demands."

The people of Punjab, Haryana, and the whole country want that there should be peace, there should be an atmosphere of harmony, but a small minority is against this. She said that among those people who are trying to create an atmosphere of terror in Punjab, most are criminals, smugglers, anti-national elements, and some foreign agents. These foreign agents are giving these people weapons and money. They are coming into this country in disguise. These people indulge in breakage and terrorising of people. The people's cooperation is needed in every village to catch these people. This is not the police's work only.

It is said that huge numbers of people of the neighbouring country Pakistan have entered the country in the disguise of Sikhs.

Mrs. Gandhi said that the biggest problem was that the Akalis did not remain firm on anything. Mrs. Gandhi said, "Recently when most of the religious demands of the Akalis were accepted, they had objections to the fact that the announcement of accepting their demands was made in the gurudwaras?"

A strange kind of perplexity came on the face of the Prime Minister. Describing this incident, she said, "It was not my intention to say this there, but I happened to go to the gurudwara and there someone asked me about this, so I said this."

Here, she also made it clear that it was not possible for her to accept every demand of theirs. She had to think not only on Punjab, but about the other states also. She had been trying continuously to solve the problem, but she neither believed in getting any of her demands accepted by force nor did she accept anybody else's demands due to pressure.

During the course of the whole conversation, she looked very worried and her face was a picture of sensitivity and deep emotions. Once she said, "Is it necessary that if we meet someone or talk to someone, it is only with some motive." Her belief was that, "People meet each other and sit together sometimes purely on a humanitarian basis also. But, it always happens that I agree to meet them and the Akalis shirk from meeting me. Sometimes they cite one reason and sometimes they cite another reason for not meeting me."

On my saying that if they are not ready to meet you, then this fact must be brought before the people, Mrs. Gandhi said – "This work should be done by the media. They should bring the truth before the people because there is no lack of such opposition parties also who are giving the whole issue a communal look due to their limited interests and selfishness, without thinking what the results of such an action would be. Due to this, the unity of the country can be in danger and some foreign powers can take benefit of such a situation."

Sant Harchand Singh Longowal says that the representatives of the Sikhs had refused to sign the Constitution in 1948 because at that time also their objection to Article 25 of the Constitution was not listened to. The question is that if this Article was so objectionable then why was no serious demand raised to change it or to make it more balanced for 35 long years?

Dr. Rafiq Zakaria told an even more surprising thing recently in the Parliament. He said that the Akali leader, Sant Harchand Singh Longowal, had declared the information given by Mrs. Indira Gandhi in the Lok Sabha to be false. The information given by Mrs. Indira Gandhi in the Lok Sabha was that years before Master Tarasingh had given his acceptance to Sardar Patel on the issue of Article 25 and of keeping the Sikhs together with the Hindus. Dr. Zakaria said clearly in his statement that possibly Sant Longowal was not fully aware of all the facts. After this, he described in detail about the Constituent Assembly and the talks that had been held with the Sikh representatives at that time.

It is very clear from the above description that Sant Longowal was probably not aware of the full facts. Even otherwise, it is not difficult to understand from the meaning that the thinkers have derived of Article 25 and the description that they have given of its influence, that the above Article not only ensures a separate identity for the Sikhs, but also ensures full rights for them.

It is a matter of surprise and sadness that the responsible leadership of Akali Dal has taken such steps due to which the problem got more complex. It would have been better if the Akali leadership had brought about such a situation in which the whole problem would have been solved in an atmosphere of empathy and sensitivity. Instead, whatever has happened during the last few months puts a big question mark on the appropriateness of the movement.

It was Mrs. Gandhi's clear decision about the Anandpur proposal that it was not acceptable to her and the Akalis would also have to leave it because there were a lot of issues in it, like the issue of Ganga Nagar, which could not be accepted at any cost.

Replying to another question, the Prime Minister said – "There are a lot of 'national minorities' in India like Sikhs, Muslims, Parsis,

Christians, Buddhists etc., but we all are tied by one word 'Indians'. The amount of facilities that are given to the minorities in India are probably not given to any minority community in any country of the world."

On the question of Chandigarh, the Prime Minister was of the opinion, "Personally, I am committed to giving Chandigarh to Punjab. But, the matter does not end here. First, Haryana should agree to this. There are many aspects to this issue. There is the issue of Abohar and Fazilka. The Akalis have still not agreed that Abohar and Fazilka and its adjoining areas should be given to Haryana."

The way in which Mrs. Gandhi thinks about Haryana in the whole context, and the way in which she thinks about national interest; this way of thinking is a matter of relief for all those who believe in national unity and democracy. I remembered an incident, which reminded me how complex this problem is. I told Mrs. Indira Gandhi of this incident. During my recent trip to Mumbai, I saw that people shirked from sitting in taxis which had Sikh drivers. Whereas, till a few days ago, the situation was such that if the driver of the taxi was a Sikh, then people felt relieved. They felt that even if they sent their sisters and daughters alone in the taxi, they would be safe. What an unbreakable faith they had in their Sikh brothers!

This atmosphere of suspicion was spreading fast into the other parts of the country due to the violent incidents happening in Punjab and Haryana. If this situation was allowed to develop, then what would the future be like could be imagined very well by everybody.

On hearing about the above incident, Mrs. Gandhi's reaction was, "The need of the hour is that our Sikh brothers who are against violence, who are living in Punjab and outside Punjab, should collect together and put pressure on the terrorists and tell their opinion to the people in a collective way." She was of the opinion that the newspapers could help a lot in bringing about the right atmosphere. If people went to Punjab and Haryana and took part in the 'peace marches' then it would help a lot in bringing about the right atmosphere.

In this interview, which lasted for about an hour, I was able to feel the Prime Minister's worry about this problem and her heartfelt desire to solve this problem quickly. During the interview, Mrs. Gandhi said, "The sants give out a '*hukamnama*' (order). I can't give out a '*hukamnama*' because I am not a dictator. I have to think about the whole country."

I felt that Mrs. Gandhi was very saddened at the incidents taking place in the country, but she was also determined to put an end to these activities very soon so that the country could move forward. But, she wanted the support of all the people, especially the media, artistes, and the intellectuals in this effort."

It is obvious from this conversation that Punjab had been brought to a very bad situation. The whole of Punjab was crying out in pain at the behaviour of the Akalis, the activities of the terrorists, and the sufferings of the common man; and no solution to the problem seemed to be in sight.

It was very clear that Indira Gandhi had wanted to take part in peace talks many times, but it seemed that the Akalis had no interest in a compromise, and they wanted to keep protesting just for the sake of it. Punjab was burning due to this, terrorist activities were growing, and the anti-national elements were becoming active.

The Prime Minister was very worried, undoubtedly. The leaders of the opposition were demanding that the continuously deteriorating situation in Punjab be brought under control and that some action be taken against the terrorists.

Indira Gandhi had tried a lot to solve the problem through talks and she was not able to understand what to do now to make the situation normal.

The biggest worry was that all the big leaders of the Akali Dal had become silent and were not ready to cooperate even a little bit in the fight against terrorism. The premises of the Golden Temple had become a centre for military training and, in the big rooms inside, weapons and ammunition were being accumulated.

Whenever the terrorists needed money, they would attack a bank and would loot as much money as they wanted. If anyone dared to speak against them, he would be shot openly in broad daylight. The victims of the terrorists were the common people, the journalists, and the opposition leaders also.

There are no two opinions about the fact that if a strong step had not been taken in Punjab then there would have been a lot of bloodshed there. When the Akali Dal did not take any step to remove the terrorists from the Golden Temple premises, then the Central Government had no other option left but to take a strong step – they gave the orders for the army to march to Amritsar.

13

MILITARY ACTION AGAINST TERRORISTS

Before the start of the military action to flush out terrorists from the Golden Temple premises, Indira Gandhi had accepted helplessly that there were some decisions that one had to take against one's wishes because it was necessary to take these decisions for the benefit of the common people.

Indira Gandhi knew very well that if she gave the order for the army to be sent to the Golden Temple, she would have to become a target of the wrath of a very big section of the people. She would have to listen to their bitter criticism and would perhaps even be deprived of their votes. But, still she took this step. Even this truth could not shake her from her path that due to this step the religious feelings of some people could be hurt, and that some selfish people could take advantage of this situation.

There were two options before her – let the situation remain as it was or take the correct step without any hesitation.

It was correct that the whole of Punjab was suffering due to the activities of the terrorists. The administration had come to a standstill. The law and order situation had become very bad. The students' studies were suffering. Business institutions were lying closed and the economy of the state was in a bad shape. The attendance in offices and factories had become very low and there was almost no work being done in them. The transport situation was in shambles. The buses used to stop plying in the evenings. Even in the cities, women did not dare to venture out of their houses – especially at night, and all this was due to the terrorists.

For how long could any responsible government tolerate a situation like this? Indira Gandhi had given many chances to the Akali Dal and to the terrorists, but there was no change in their attitudes.

The terrorists used to hide in the Golden Temple because they believed that no action would be taken against them as long as they were there. Neither could the police come in and catch them, nor could the jawans of the army. After all, who would tolerate it if the police or the army came into the Golden Temple? If they came in, then the purity of the Golden Temple would be destroyed, which nobody would be able to tolerate.

This thinking of theirs was completely wrong. Actually, the purity of the Golden Temple had already been destroyed because of their presence. Nowadays, the previous gaiety could not be seen in the Golden Temple. Every other day, a murder was committed in its premises. Due to the weapons and ammunition that had been collected there and due to the illegal activities that were being carried out there, the grandeur, grace, serenity, and purity of the Golden Temple had been destroyed and this fact was also no less painful for Indira Gandhi.

Now, there was only one option left before Indira Gandhi, and this was the first painful decision that she had to take in her life.

In the first week of June, she gave the orders to the army to enter the Golden Temple and to remove the terrorists from there.

The orders had been given to the army that while tackling the terrorists, care should be taken that not even a single bullet should be fired towards the main building of the Golden Temple.

The army followed the orders of the government to the letter.

After entering the Golden Temple, the army had to face a very big opposition from the terrorists who were armed with the latest weapons. The army had not expected such strong opposition from the terrorists.

The terrorists had converted the Golden Temple into a fortress and they fought back bitterly.

The army did not want to spill blood. It first advised the terrorists to surrender. When the terrorists did not agree to this, then the army launched their attack against them.

It was not easy for the army to defeat the terrorists. The terrorists were holed up in the Golden Temple in such a place from where they could see the activities of the army men clearly. Most of the bullets were being fired from the main building of the Golden Temple, where the government had forbidden the army to fire even a single bullet.

In order to enter the Golden Temple premises and capture the terrorists, the army had to cross through a shower of bullets being fired by the terrorists. Many of their soldiers were killed due to this, but the army was successful in entering the temple and in taking positions there. It was an incomparable example of their dedication to duty that even when a shower of bullets was being fired at them from the main building of the Golden Temple, not even a single jawan fired a bullet in that direction.

In this military action, in the end, the terrorists had to bow before the army. Their leaders, Bhindrawale and Amrik Singh, were killed during the military operation and the terrorists were cleared from the Golden Temple.

The army found a huge cache of weapons in the Golden Temple– both Indian and foreign made. Some were China and Pakistan made. Besides the weapons, they also found foreign currency and objectionable documents. They also found a lot of money, gold etc. In one room, they even found a small factory of weapons.

There was a very strong reaction against the military action in the Golden Temple. The Sikhs felt themselves to be victimised. The people connected with the party were angry with Indira Gandhi. But, the Golden Temple had been freed of the terrorists, which was definitely beneficial for the nation in all ways.

Many people have said many things about what happened in the Golden Temple. Presented here are the thoughts of Jagjit Singh

Arora. It was under his leadership that the army got victory in Bangladesh and the army of West Pakistan was forced to surrender. His thoughts –

"The army was able to do very well the work which was given to it, with full military decorum and traditions. But, the feeling of happiness that one gets on being victorious against the enemies is not there when fighting against one's own people. One has to fight against one's own people when there are no other options left. Despite this, everyone should feel proud of the self-control showed by the army.

"In spite of this, the feelings of the Sikhs have been hurt by the army's entry into the Golden Temple. It would have been better if the Golden Temple had been freed from the terrorists in the same way in which the gurudwara in Moga was freed – by the use of pressure by the semi-military forces. It would have been a long and tiring activity, but the common Sikhs would not have felt humiliated due to this.

"The government is guilty for this situation. Sant Jarnail Singh Bhindrawale was a product of the Congress whom they had used in the elections of 1980. Actually, the Central Government has always kept their hand on Sant Bhindrawale's shoulders. If this hand had been kept on the shoulder of Sant Longowal, then such a situation would not have arisen. Prime Minister Mrs. Indira Gandhi has refuted this allegation in an interview with a correspondent of the B.B.C. and called it baseless. The common Sikh is peace-loving and hard-working. He does not have time for any useless fights. Where was the need for the government to keep Sant Bhindrawale, who had been caught for Lala Jagat Narain's murder, in a rest house instead of a prison? Then, it released Sant Bhindrawale saying that it had not been able to gather proof against him. If it had to do all this, then what was the need to take him into custody? Even after that, Bhindrawale used to roam in Mumbai and Delhi fully armed, but neither was an eye kept on him nor was he caught. When he made his base in the Golden Temple, then they raised a commotion.

"I believe that a little understanding by the government and a more flexible policy would have won over the Sikhs forever. But the 'obstinate policy' of both of them harmed the common Sikhs. I have never supported this idea that fully armed people should roam about openly in the Golden Temple. I had even said in a religious meeting in the Golden Temple that if you show off your weapons to the people openly like this, then the people will lose their faith in the Sikh religion, the religion which has come into existence after a lot of sacrifices. I had criticised Bhindrawale's violent activities openly. But, I definitely had to face some discomfort at the time when during the broadcast of a programme from All India Radio, I was instructed clearly that I could use the words terrorist and terrorism, but I should not mention the name of Sant Bhindrawale anywhere.

"The situation will improve if an appeal is made by the President and the Sikh '*granthis*' but it will take some time. The appeal that the President made to the nation 10 days after the incident, if he had made that appeal before, it would have had some effect. The Prime Minister should also have come on the radio and television because she was the one who made the announcement of giving military support to the administration. The Akalis and the '*jathedars*' are also to blame. It is correct that the government should have been more alert when the weapons were coming into the Golden Temple in an illegal manner, but what were the Gurudwara Prabandhak Committee and the Akali leaders doing at that time? Why did they allow the holy place to become a military cantonment? The second question is why was Bhindrawale given permission to live in the Akal Takht? The Akal Takht is also a holy place like Harminder Sahib. Nobody has ever lived there, not even Maharaja Ranjit Singh. Nobody knows under what pressure Tohra Sahib gave the permission to Sant Bhindrawale and his supporters to live there. Once Sant Bhindrawale had established his base there, then it was not possible for the Akali leaders to remove him from there. When the army had to work so hard to remove the terrorists and so many jawans and officers of the army had to sacrifice their lives to remove the terrorists from there, then how could Sant Longowal and the other Akali leaders have been able to remove the terrorists from there?

"As regards the question of the Sikh deserters from the army, this was a reaction to the situation that was prevailing at that time; it was not a planned conspiracy. If it had been a conspiracy, then those people would have run away from the army with their weapons and in their uniforms. But, these people were captured midway only. It was good that they were captured. Due to their capture, there is no fear of any type of indiscipline coming into the army. Our army has its own tradition. Here, the Sikhs may have to face mistrust for some time. They will have to regain the trust of the army and the government once again.

"At this time, the necessity is for the Sikhs to keep religion and politics separate. Actually, if religion and politics come together, then problems always arise. Politics is always flexible, whereas religion is unchanging. So, this is a good opportunity for the Sikhs to free themselves from the '*jathedars*' and to hand over the reins of their future into the hands of educated and wise people. Now, the times have changed and only those religions can be successful the reins of which are in the hands of enlightened and farsighted people. The government should not take over the responsibility of the reconstruction of the Golden Temple in its hands, but '*kar seva*' should be done. Baba Harbans Singh has seen the Golden Temple himself and he seems to be ready to take over the responsibility of the '*kar seva*'. A lot of workers will be needed to complete this '*kar seva*'. To maintain the Hindu-Sikh unity, it is necessary that both the religions establish a joint trust so that the affected families can be helped. The government is helping the soldiers, but besides that the families of the other people who were killed should also be helped.

"This logic is wrong that due to the present action, the foundation of Khalistan will be laid. We should not think like this at all. It is dangerous to even bring this thought into our minds.

Khalistan is a cancer, which will eat away the whole Sikh community. So, no Sikh should even bring this word on his lips."

It is obvious from these thoughts of Jagjit Singh Arora that whatever happened was very unfortunate and that this should not have happened. But, because there was no other option except this, the government was forced to take this step.

Due to this action of the government, the Sikh brothers were hurt in their most tender spot. Everyone thought that it was a very unfortunate thing that the army had to be sent to a religious place like the Golden Temple and that the religious feelings of the Sikhs were hurt due to this, and they felt insulted due to this. The feeling of the Sikhs was that due to this military action, the purity of their religious place had been violated. Whereas the government was of the opinion that due to this action, the purity of the Golden Temple was not sullied, but was restored. The purity of the holy place had already been destroyed by the activities of the terrorists and their presence in the Golden Temple, and the government had attempted to bring it back by the military action. Yes, the government had also accepted that the decision to send the army into the Golden Temple was a very difficult decision for it to take and some of the actions that had to be taken there were very regrettable.

Indira Gandhi herself was very saddened by this situation. She had tried very hard to bring the feelings of the Sikh community under control.

A lot of damage to life and property had been caused due to the military action. Both armymen and the terrorists had been killed in large numbers in this action. The terrorists had faced the army with their full strength. They had converted the whole Golden Temple into an impenetrable fortress. They had done more firing from the main building of the Golden Temple so that the army could be stopped from coming inside. The terrorists knew that due to religious reasons the army would not lift its rifles in the direction of the main building and neither would it attack that area. They were right. The army really did not fire even a single bullet in that direction and quietly faced the bullets of the terrorists that were being fired from there on their chests. Due to this, many soldiers of the army were killed.

In this action, except the main building, many buildings of the Golden Temple were damaged. Heavy firing had been done from both the sides.

In the end, the terrorists were driven away from the Golden Temple and the holy place was freed from them. From the cache of illegal weapons and the other material that was obtained from there, it was evident that the intentions of the terrorists were not good and large-scale preparations were being made to carry out some big conspiracy. It was also evident that the terrorists had links with the outside enemies.

The army was not removed from the Golden Temple immediately after the military action. To maintain peace, the army was stationed there for some time, whereas the demand of the chief '*granthis*' and the other Akali officials was that the army be removed from the Golden Temple immediately. This was not possible immediately because illegal materials were being found continuously in the Golden Temple premises and it was thought that if the army went away from there, the remaining terrorists would gather there again. The peace that had been obtained at a heavy cost could be lost again.

The army had spread all over Punjab in search of the remaining terrorists. In cities, villages, and in big gurudwaras, the terrorists were being captured in large numbers. In many places, the peace-loving citizens themselves gave the information to the army about the presence of the terrorists, and themselves gathered illegal weapons from the gurudwaras and other places and handed them over to the army.

Besides all this, the government was continuing its efforts to lessen the pain that had been caused to the Sikh community and to heal its wounds.

In this connection, Indira Gandhi had given a statement. The President also gave a statement in this connection that was very emotional.

The President had said –

"India's history has been such that the people of all castes, religions, and communities have lived here together. But, these days, the people have become victims of misunderstandings. The crack that is caused in the relations between people of two communities is usually caused due to misunderstandings. Actually, this crack forms in the relations of the people of two communities due to people who spread wrong information. The people should try to establish an atmosphere of mutual respect, brotherhood, and tolerance so that the people can remove their misunderstandings. The people should try to establish an atmosphere of love instead of hatred so that they can win over the faith of the people who are victims of misunderstanding. The truth is that all religions are like members of one family. All religions are like branches of one plant. It is the responsibility of the whole nation to maintain patriotism, nationalism, and secularism.

"Countrymen! The blood of Sikhs and Hindus is one, their environment is one, their living is one, their relations are one, their tears are one, and their laughter is also one. But a time came, when the tears belonged to someone else, and the laughter belonged to someone else. This had never happened before. I want the earlier time to come once more when our laughter and tears are one.

"All religions have grown in the lap of Mother India. All our religious places are here, the saints and holy men of our country are here, our brave soldiers are here, our scientists and doctors are here, our working class people are here, our big officers, our farmers and labourers are here. It is our duty to think about the sufferings of all these people as our own suffering. I want to appeal to everyone to walk on the path of unity, to talk about compromise. We should not only talk about compromise, but we should make goodwill committees and try to inculcate a feeling of unity in the people. If someone has made a mistake and is now asking for forgiveness for those mistakes, then we should forgive him. All of us are the residents of this country, we are the sons and daughters of this country. It is our duty to ensure that our Mother India does not suffer anymore.

"My dear countrymen! The great guru of our country, 'Sache Badshahji' has given us the teaching that whatever religion a person may follow, whatever may be the traditions and rituals of that religion, whatever may be the method of his offering prayers, the God that they are praying to is one."

This appeal of Giani Zail Singh was very emotional. It had come out from the depth of his heart. The whole nation listened with great attention to this appeal of his. The nation got the message that it should try to forget whatever had happened and should try to establish brotherhood and goodwill again.

The first thing that was necessary was that the Golden Temple, which had been badly damaged due to the military action, should be repaired. Presently, the entry of devotees to the Golden Temple had been stopped. The government wanted to first bring the Golden Temple back to its original state, and then open its doors for the devotees.

The repair of the Golden Temple was possible only by religious rules and traditions. Whenever repair or construction of the Sikh gurudwaras is done, it is by '*kar seva*' only. '*Kar seva*' means that all people who wish to take part in the construction or repair of the holy place, no matter to which religion they might belong, themselves come up and offer their services to repair or construct the holy place. All the work is done in the form of a voluntary service and, whatever money is spent, is obtained by donations. The government wanted that '*kar seva*' should start in the Golden Temple as soon as possible and the previous prestige of the holy place should be restored. For this, an appeal was made to the chief '*granthis*' that they should make efforts to hasten the start of the '*kar seva*'.

But, this did not happen. The Akali officials and the chief '*granthis*' of the Golden Temple had no enthusiasm towards the '*kar seva*'. They wanted the Golden Temple to remain in that condition. There was a possibility that the condition would deteriorate further due to this. The government requested many big Sikh leaders and '*sants*' to begin the '*kar seva*', but nobody was ready to do this due to some reason. Some people were ready and wanted to start the '*kar seva*', but nobody wanted to become the target of the wrath of the chief '*granthis*'.

In such a situation, the first person to agree to do the '*kar seva*' was the '*nihang sant*' Sant Singh. The '*nihangs*' had always taken part in the '*kar seva*' in the gurudwaras and the holy places– this is a historical truth. Carrying this tradition forward, they decided to start the '*kar seva*' in the Golden Temple. The chief '*granthis*' and the leaders of the Akali Dal opposed this vehemently, but none of them were able to deter Baba Sant Singh and his followers from taking part in this holy work.

Baba Sant Singh started the '*kar seva*' with his followers according to the traditions. Lakhs of Hindus and Sikhs took part in this work. In this way, the repair work of the Golden Temple was started in a planned and organised way.

14

REACTIONS

There was a strong reaction to the action taken in the Golden Temple. There were hundreds of false rumours floating around. There were doubts in the minds of the common Sikh population. Even the Sikhs who were in the army had been provoked by vested elements. The revolt by the Sikhs in the army was suppressed with strictness.

It would not be correct to think that the whole Sikh community had reacted negatively to this action. The truth was that the positive-minded Sikhs believed that the government had taken the right step in taking military action against the anti-national elements. If the government had not taken this strong step, then chaos and lawlessness would have spread in the whole of Punjab and the effect of this on the entire nation would also have been very bad. In the military action in the Golden Temple, many Sikhs had also taken part. Everyone had been saddened by the action that had been taken in the Golden Temple. Even the army had hesitated a little in taking this action. But, keeping in mind the good of the entire nation, they entered the Golden Temple with a heavy heart. At that time, prayers were on their lips. It was only a very small section of the Sikh community that was showing political opposition against this action.

White paper

The government had published a white paper on the military action taken in Punjab to remove many of the suspicions and doubts from the minds of the people. Due to this white paper, the doubts of many people were resolved and many false rumours that were floating around in the country were put to rest.

In the white paper, the government had given a stepwise description of the action taken in Punjab, due to which the situation became clearer to many common people.

As was evident from the white paper, it was not the intention of the government, in taking the military action, to hurt the feelings of the Sikh community. But, the government itself was very saddened because the feelings of the Sikh community had been hurt by this action. The government was also surprised by the fact that no one was thinking about the fact that the sanctity of the Golden Temple was harmed more by the terrorists taking shelter in the temple premises. What other option did the government have to stop the reign of terror and murder that the terrorists had spread in Punjab? Undoubtedly, if the Akali Dal and the chief '*granthis*' had cooperated with the government in the beginning and had taken action against the terrorists, then possibly, the government would not have been compelled to take such a strong action.

Sant Bhindrawale was delivering provocative speeches daily from the Golden Temple, and those Akali officials and sants, on whose shoulders the responsibility for the protection of the Golden Temple was, were sitting silently. The truth was that the entire Akali Dal had become directionless and had bowed its head in front of the terrorists. In such a situation, it was felt that military action was the only method of solving the problem.

The government issued the white paper on 10 July. In this, a datewise description of all the incidents in Punjab was given. It said that the government had not adopted the policy of offence, but had adopted a policy of self-defence. It was said that the terrorists were receiving active support in cash and kind from some foreign elements. The government had definite proof of all this, but keeping in mind the good of the public, it was not disclosing the names of the national and foreign entities. Before the white paper had been issued, there had been many statements by the government and non-government bodies about the fact that the terrorists had support from the foreign elements. But, the fact that the names of these elements were not mentioned in the white paper could give rise to many types of stories and conjectures.

Despite this shortcoming, the white paper was an important document. In this 165-page document, the detailed description of the Punjab revolution along with documentary proof was given – how the movement of the Akali Dal slowly adopted communal colours, how the separatists and the terrorists came to have a strong influence on the Akali Dal, how this movement slowly adopted an anti-national form due to the intrusion of the criminals, smugglers, anti-social elements, and the naxalites.

It was said in the white paper that the Shiromani Akali Dal had started the movement in September 1981, but slowly the threads of the movements slipped out of its hands. In the white paper, there was no direct mention of the support of any foreign government, but detailed description was given of the activities of parties like the Dal Khalsa, Babbar Khalsa, Akhand Kirtani Jatha, and Khalistan in countries like America, Britain, Canada, West Germany, and Holland. Despite a letter of protest by the government, the activities of the self-proclaimed leader of Khalistan, Dr. Jagjit Singh Chauhan, who declared that he had the support of many American senators, were not stopped. Dr. Chauhan was allowed entry into countries like America and Canada. The Dal Khalsa had openly declared Pakistan as its social friend; and it was the claim of Dr. Chauhan that Pakistani soldiers in the guise of Sikhs, were stationed at Guru Ramdas Sarai and they were under the control of Sant Bhindrawale.

There were five chapters in the white paper in which the demands of the Akalis, terrorism and violence, the military action, and the issues that arose due to the activities of the terrorists, were discussed. There were many schedules and pictures of the fortification of the Golden Temple were also given in this white paper. Before asking for military help, the government had tried to find a solution to the problem by talks with the Akali leadership. It had become absolutely necessary to take the help of the army to remove the terrorists from the Golden Temple and from other places because there was a danger to the security, unity, and integrity of the country from them. It was no longer possible for the ordinary agencies responsible for law and order to deal with these terrorists.

The white paper also threw light on all the issues involved with the Anandpur Sahib proposal and the thoughts and the demands of the Akalis. On making Amritsar a holy city, the reaction of the government was that to give any city such a status would be to disregard the secular structure of our Constitution. The government was ready to give Amritsar the status that it had given to Haridwar or Kurukshetra, under which the local administration could put a stop to the sale of meat and liquor. But, the Akali party was not interested in this. The government said that installing a transmitter in the Golden Temple for the broadcasting of '*shabd kirtan*' was against national policies. It put forward the proposal of increasing the duration of the '*kirtan*' on Akashvani to 90 minutes, but the Akali party did not budge from its demand of a broadcast of three hours' duration. The government was ready to give permission to the Sikhs to carry a '*kirpan*' of a certain length on domestic flights, but it expressed its inability to allow the Sikhs to carry the '*kirpan*' on Air India flights, due to the international rules, which forbid the carrying of weapons on flights.

Regarding the question of the All India Gurudwara Act, it was said in the white paper that the government had to look after the interests of other people and state governments also. The administrators of the gurudwaras, which were outside Punjab, did not want to come under the Shiromani Gurudwara Prabandhak Committee. Therefore, the government could not agree to this Act.

Regarding the river water dispute, the Akali Dal had adopted an inflexible and obstinate approach. In the beginning, the Akali Dal was in favour of handing over the Ravi, Vyas water dispute to the tribunal, but later it changed its stance. The Akali Dal now made the demand that the tribunal should be asked to work on the basis of the 1955 agreement and not the December 1981 agreement. The Prime Minister assured the Akali leaders that their interests would not be neglected. In spite of this, the attitude of the Akali Dal did not change. Regarding the question of land, the Prime Minister had said time and again that Chandigarh would be given to Punjab, if Harayana got the Hindi-speaking areas of Punjab as compensation. But, the Akali Dal wanted that Chandigarh should be given to them, but the responsibility for deciding about all other disputed regions should be handed over to the tribunal. Thus, there was a conflict on this issue also.

Some fundamental questions were also raised in the white paper. Was it justifiable that the places of worship, where lakhs of people offered prayers, should be used as arsenals of weapons? Was it justifiable that these places were made shelter homes for the criminals and anti-social elements? The finding of weapons in large quantities, instruments of communication, and the factories of weapons in the Golden Temple premises show what the final goal of the terrorists was. Their final goal was to launch a reign of terror and to launch large-scale destruction to achieve their objective of separatism. In front of the eyes of the Akali Dal and the Shiromani Gurudwara Prabandhak Committee, the material for spreading terror was being gathered, but they did not raise their voice against this. The Shiromani Gurudwara Prabandhak Committee is legally responsible for the administration of the gurudwaras. The Akali party has made full use of the religious symbols and traditions to carry its movement forward. During this time, the fanatical elements grew and prospered. It was also said in the white paper that the military action was not against the Sikhs, but was against terrorism and separatism.

It was also described in the white paper how the attitude of the revolutionaries slowly became violent. In April 1978, due to the struggle with the '*nirankaris*' and afterwards, due to their religious leader, Baba Gurbachan Singh's assassination, the tension between the two communities grew. After that, the religious violence grew continuously and the slogans of the All India Sikh Students' Federation and '*Khalistan Zindabad*' were heard frequently. Lala Jagat Narain who raised his voice against the killing of the '*nirankaris*' also became a victim of the bullets of the terrorists. After this, the hijacking of the Indian Airlines aeroplane and taking it to Lahore; the assassination of police D.I.G., Atwal; and the terrorism training being given in terrorist-training camps were some of the incidents which encouraged the separatist forces in the country. How afterwards the terrorists indulged in a campaign of killing people belonging to a particular religion was also described in the white paper.

In the white paper, the government had cleared the situation from its side, but the Akali leaders completely rejected these arguments of the government.

Finally, the reconstruction of the Golden Temple by '*kar seva*' was completed and its previous glory and magnificence was restored. Due to the tireless efforts by Baba Santa Singh, this great work was completed. This work was praised everywhere. In the 'Sarbat Khalsa' conference that was held in Punjab on the completion of this work, this work of Baba Santa Singh was publicly honoured.

The Golden Temple was then handed over to the chief 'granthis' and the officials of the Golden Temple.

The situation was relatively peaceful now. The terrorist activities in Punjab had stopped completely. Now, only one task was left. This was to console those Sikh brothers who felt angry and hurt due to this military action.

This was possible only by inculcating the feeling of brotherhood and goodwill.

Indira Gandhi, herself went to Punjab and prayed at the Golden Temple. A very big task had been accomplished and the entire nation was heaving a sigh of relief, but it could be seen clearly that day that Indira Gandhi was worried. The sole reason for her worry was how to fill the cracks that had formed in the hearts of the Sikhs.

She had a very deep relation with the Sikhs. She had done a

lot for the progress and development of Punjab. She was an admirer of the bravery and patriotism of the Punjabis. The entire nation held the Sikh community in great respect. Everyone knew that in times of trouble the Sikhs had always come forward to serve the nation. Indira Gandhi wanted that a feeling of self-confidence and enthusiasm should be infused into the Sikh community as quickly as possible so that they would no longer feel themselves to be alone.

She was able to achieve this to a great extent. The majority of the Sikhs supported her. There were some selfish elements who were angry with Indira Gandhi for this action, but the support of the majority of the Sikhs was with her.

But, it is always the selfish elements who win, because they attack stealthily. These selfish elements, to whichever religion or community they may belong, their goal is only one – commitment to a narrow and fanatical ideology.

Whatever Indira Gandhi did was for the welfare of the vast majority of Sikhs. She was never in favour of pleasing a small group of people for her own selfish motives. She worked to achieve the goal of brotherhood, goodwill, and religious tolerance. It was difficult for Indira Gandhi to tolerate the barrier that the selfish elements tried to construct between the Hindu and the Sikh community. National unity and integrity was an important issue in her eyes. She took that strong step to preserve national unity and integrity, and she sacrificed her life also for national unity and integrity.

15

ON THAT WEDNESDAY...

It was the morning of Wednesday 31 October 1984.

The usual activity could be seen in the Prime Minister's house at 1, Safdarjung Road. Actually, 1, Safdarjung Road seemed a little busier than usual because the Prime Minister had returned from a tour of Orissa the previous day.

The atmosphere was a little depressed and fearful. A sense of foreboding filled the people at 1, Safdarjung Road.

Very soon, the Prime Minister was going to come out of her house. Her bodyguards and the security people were waiting for her outside, fully alert. Due to the unfortunate incidents that had happened in the country lately, the danger to the Prime Minister's life had increased and the arrangements for her security had been tightened.

When the Prime Minister awoke in the morning, she was feeling refreshed and energetic as always. Her face had a special glow and her eyes had a special light, as if she had seen some invisible thing, which only she could see, and the other people were unaware of.

In one room, the T.V. people were sitting. The Prime Minister met them at the appointed time. Her make-up was done for a T.V. shooting.

The Irish-West German television was making a serial on her. The director of the serial, Peter Ustinov, and his team were waiting for her in the 1, Akbar Road office. This place was only 100 yards away from the Prime Minister's residence. After doing her make-up, the Prime Minister had to go there.

When she emerged from the make-up room wearing a saffron-coloured saree, she was looking very radiant. She had always been beautiful, but today her beauty seemed more captivating. What was the reason behind this? Although nobody else knew, it was evident from the slight smile on her face that she knew very well what fate had in store for her.

She came out of her house at around 8:30 a.m.

From her house, a narrow lane went towards 1, Akbar Road. If the Prime Minister wanted, she could go by car also, but the distance was so less that usually she used to walk across. The Prime Minister's residence and office were side-by-side and they were separated by a small wall between them. But, the compounds of the two buildings were common. After the shooting, the Prime Minister had to go to her office in South Block.

The usual crowd was not present that day at the Akbar Road office. The daily programme that was held there in which the Prime Minister met the common people every morning had been cancelled that day. That morning, the time had been allotted to the film people, who had even gone to Bhubaneshwar (Orissa) with her.

Seeing the Prime Minister outside, the security personnel got alert.

The Prime Minister glanced around her and then walked with quick steps towards the small lane. Behind her were five security personnel who were being led by the Personal Security Officer, Dinesh Bhatt. These people were at a distance of two or three yards from the Prime Minister.

Following behind was the Prime Minister's Personal Secretary, R.K. Dhawan.

The Sun that had arisen from the east direction had not risen very high up (or maybe, it did not want to rise very high up). The beginning of the winter season could be felt.

The Prime Minister was walking calmly and fearlessly. What was she thinking at that time? Definitely, she was thinking about the country, about the unity of the country, about religious goodwill, about religious tolerance, about the progress of the country, about the security of the country, about the independence of South Africa, about the unceasing struggle of the Palestine Liberation Organisation, about the tension in international politics, and many other problems like this. Because she was the Prime Minister, it was only natural that she would be thinking about these problems. But, she was not only the Prime Minister, she was also an aware and sensitive human being. So, she used to not only think, but also used to worry. Worry – that showed that she was constantly trying to be true to her responsibilities.

But, at this time also was she thinking this only, or something else? Was she thinking about her life or maybe even her death?

Maybe not. She had dedicated her life to the nation, then why would she think about it now? And death? If she had ever thought about that, then she would have never taken such fearless decisions. But, whenever the question of the unity of the nation arose, she would not flinch on even seeing death in front of her. What is death? It has to come one day, but death itself salutes those people who die to protect their ideals.

Only yesterday, she had said in a public meeting in Orissa, "If even the last drop of my blood comes to the aid of my nation, then I will consider myself fortunate."

She was ever ready to sacrifice her life if her life could in any way help the nation. She was living for those high ideals, which she had imbibed from Gandhi, Nehru, Ashok, and Akbar.

Walking fast, the Prime Minister reached near the main gate. Nobody knew that an extremely unfortunate incident was going to take place in the next few minutes.

When the Prime Minister reached the main gate, suddenly two security men who were crouching behind the bougainvillea plant got up. One was on the right side of the lane and the other one was on the left side of the lane.

The Prime Minister knew both these men well. On the right side stood Sub-Inspector Beant Singh, and on the left side stood

Constable Satwant Singh. Beant Singh had been working in the Prime Minister's residence since eight long years and the Prime Minister held him in great regard. Both the bodyguards stood with their back to Safdarjung Road and they were looking towards the Prime Minister who was coming towards them.

The time was 9:18 in the morning.

Suddenly, the peaceful atmosphere was shattered by the sound of bullets.

Nobody was able to understand what had happened. Everyone was shocked by the blasts and by the time they could understand what was happening, it was already too late.

There was a sten gun in the hands of Constable Satwant Singh. When he had lifted his sten gun in the direction of the Prime Minister, the other bodyguards had thought that he was saluting the Prime Minister – but only for a little while. As soon as the constable pressed the trigger, a shower of bullets riddled the body of the Prime Minister. The Prime Minister keeled over. Then, Beant Singh who was standing at a little distance, fired five shots into the Prime Minister's body from his revolver. The Prime Minister fell unconscious. Maybe, even as she was falling, this thought was in her mind – "Oh! Beant Singh, you too........!?"

The Prime Minister fell down unconscious. Satwant Singh had fired 14 rounds of bullets, of which 11 had hit the Prime Minister. Beant Singh had also pumped five bullets one after the other into the Prime Minister.

The area of the narrow lane where the Prime Minister had fallen was filled with blood. Her saffron-coloured saree was now soaked with blood.

When the security men who were following the Prime Minister saw this, they ran up and lifted the Prime Minister.

The Prime Minister's Press Advisor, Sharda Prasad, immediately brought his car near the Prime Minister. The Prime Minister was lifted up and put in the car. In the narrow lane, her blood-soaked slippers were lying forlorn. The other shocked and dazed security personnel came to their senses and moved forward and captured both the assassin bodyguards. Both the assassins had raised their hands in a gesture of surrender. Beant Singh announced, "I have done what I wanted to do. Now, you can do as you wish."

But, did he really know what he had done? Maybe not. He did not know what he had done. No assassin knows. All assassins think that they have done the assassination for the religion, caste, or nation, whereas the truth is that assassins have no religion, no caste, and no nation. The people who had killed the Prime Minister of India were the same who had given poison to Socrates, who had hung Jesus Christ on the Cross, who had killed Gandhi, Martin Luther King, and John Kennedy. In spite of the different nationalities and faiths, the character of all assassins is the same – narrow-minded, bitter, and fanatical.

Beant Singh tried to struggle with the security personnel and was killed by them. Satwant Singh was injured in his scuffle with the security men.

The Ambassador car that was carrying the blood-soaked body of the Prime Minister went past the main gate. Sonia Gandhi was sitting in its back seat with the Prime Minister's head on her lap. A police official and R.K. Dhawan were also in the car. Rajiv Gandhi was not in Delhi at that time. He had gone on a tour of West Bengal. Everyone's face was filled with worry. What a calamity had struck them all of a sudden!

The wounded Prime Minister was taken to the All India Institute of Medical Sciences. There, the doctors tried their best to revive the Prime Minister – but they were unsuccessful. She was immediately taken to the operating theatre, which was on the eighth floor of the hospital.

The Prime Minister lay there unmoving. Her face was without any wound, but her chest and stomach were riddled with bullets. Many instruments of life support were used, blood and glucose were given to her, oxygen was given, but all this was of no use. By that time, the Prime Minister had passed away. Her eyes were wide open.

A doctor moved forward and closed her eyes.

Darkness spread all around.

The ideals for which the Prime Minister struggled all her life, in the end, she laid down her life for those very ideals in the end.

It is said that the people who assassinated Indira Gandhi were Sikhs. But, let alone Sikhs, they were not even human beings. They were only assassins – and nothing else.

The security personnel had already become suspicious due to Beant Singh and Satwant Singh's changed attitude. That is why they had suggested to Indira Gandhi to remove them from their duty at the Prime Minister's residence. But, Indira Gandhi did not listen to them and said -- "If I do this, then how will we be able to maintain secularism in India?"

The strongest point of India's character was its secularism, then how could she let any harm come to that?

She had sacrificed her entire life in establishing a socialist and secular India.

The official news of Indira Gandhi's death was broadcast on radio and television at around 6 o'clock in the evening. But the news of her death had spread in the entire city by afternoon. And then it spread to the rest of India, and then crossing the boundaries of India, it spread to the entire world.

Suddenly, entire India was immersed in a wave of sorrow.

The people of Delhi reached the All India Institute in thousands. Everywhere men, women, and children could be seen with sad faces and wet eyes. Nobody knew what the reality was. Nobody knew whether Indira Ji was alive or not. How long would it take for her to recover? How did this incident take place? Who has killed her and why? Prayers were on everybody's lips and their hands were raised in the gesture of prayer. Some people were crying very badly, some people were silent, absolutely shocked.

When the fact of Indira Gandhi's death was corroborated, then suddenly the atmosphere of the place became very emotional. Women, men, and children were crying bitterly. People were shocked and extremely saddened by her death. It was clearly evident that the people loved Indira Gandhi a lot.

In the evening, it was announced on the radio that due to Indira Gandhi's death, a 12-day national mourning would be observed and the national flags, which were flying atop the government buildings, would fly at half-mast.

Indira Gandhi's dead body was kept in state at Teen Murti Bhavan from 1 to 3 November for people to pay their respects to her.

Presented here is the scene at Teen Murti Bhavan on 1 November 1984 –

Last journey

A huge crowd of people had gathered at Teen Murti Bhavan, New Delhi, to have the last glimpse of Indira Gandhi. People paid their last respects to Indira Gandhi with tear-filled eyes. By the time they reached the feet of the dead body, the people could not control their tears and burst into tears. Many old women and men were given support and escorted away from there because they had become very emotional on seeing Indira Gandhi's dead body.

There was a glow of infinite peace on Mrs. Indira Gandhi's face. Leaving behind lakhs and crores of weeping people, she was sleeping peacefully. Her head was covered with the '*pallav*' of an orange-coloured saree and her face was open. Slowly, the whole dead body was covered with flowers that the people put on the dead body to pay their respects. The security-men picked up the flowers and kept them separately.

In Teen Murti Bhavan, Indira Gandhi's dead body lay wrapped in the Tricolour in exactly the same way as her father, the first Prime Minister of India, Pandit Jawaharlal Nehru's body had lain on 27th May 1964.

Despite the cold, people had started gathering at the doors of Teen Murti Bhavan since the night, although they were allowed to pay their last respects to Mrs. Indira Gandhi from 7 o'clock the next morning. Even before Mrs. Indira Gandhi's dead body was brought there, long lines had formed at the place. The crowd was growing and the people who were eager to have a last glimpse of Mrs. Indira Gandhi walked quietly in lines, to pay their last respects to her.

On the roads that led to Teen Murti Bhavan, Teen Murti Marg, South Avenue, Kushak Road, and Chanakya Puri big crowds of people could be seen till late at night. The people who went to Teen Murti Bhavan by their own vehicles had to park their vehicles 1.5 kilometres away from Teen Murti Bhavan. The queues of the people went as far as Udyog Bhavan.

Priyadarshini Indira's dead body, which was wrapped up in the Tricolour, was brought to Teen Murti Bhavan at 8 o'clock in the morning. The dead body was bedecked with flowers and kept on a five-foot high stage. The new Prime Minister, Rajiv Gandhi, was standing at the feet of his mother since morning. His wife Sonia, son Rahul and daughter Priyanka were standing nearby. Rajiv was standing with folded hands, thanking the people who went by him after paying their respects.

Although, in Teen Murti Bhavan, religious prayers of all the religions were being chanted, but despite this, there was a strange kind of silence there. This silence was broken from time to time with the sound of the crying of the people or with slogans of "Long Live Indira Gandhi." The army had taken over the responsibility of management of that place.

President Giani Zail Singh reached there in the morning to pay his tributes to Mrs. Indira Gandhi. With him were his personal bodyguards. Giani Zail Singh kept a flower garland on the dead body of Mrs. Indira Gandhi and stood silently near the dead body. The Vice-President, Mr. Venkataraman, was the first leader to reach there in the morning. Mr. Rajiv Gandhi's Cabinet colleagues also remained there for a long time. Former Ministers, H.K.L. Bhagat, Shivraj Patil, and Ashok Gahlot were busy making arrangements at Teen Murti Bhavan.

Foreign citizens in large numbers, the Chief Ministers of all states, Members of Parliament, the Municipal Councillors, members of the civic bodies and many other leaders paid tributes to their departed leader with tear-filled eyes.

The former Chief Minister of Jammu and Kashmir, Farooq Abdullah; the leader of the Democratic Socialist Party, H.N. Bahuguna; the leader of Congress (S), Sharad Pawar; General Secretary, Ambika Soni and other leaders paid tributes to Mrs. Indira Gandhi.

Mrs. Indira Gandhi's maternal aunt, Mrs. Vijaylakshmi Pandit, came with her family to pay her tributes. Tears were falling from her eyes while she paid her last respects to her beloved niece.

The huge compound of Teen Murti Bhavan resounded with the cries of "Till the Sun and the Moon last, Indira, your name will remain alive," and "Long live, Indira Gandhi."

On Saturday, 3 November 1984 at 12 o'clock in the afternoon, Indira Gandhi's last journey started from Teen Murti Bhavan. Mrs. Indira Gandhi's dead body was going to be cremated at Shanti Van, which was situated on the banks of the Yamuna river. From Teen Murti to Shanti Van, the route was lined by lakhs of people who stood there to have their last glimpse of their beloved leader.

In Shanti Van, it seemed as if the entire world had gathered there. People from different parts of India, belonging to different religions, and having different languages had come there. People from many parts of the world had come there to pay their last respects. Representatives of more than 100 countries came to Indira Gandhi's funeral to pay their tributes. The Prime Minister of England, the Prime Minister of Japan, the President of Pakistan, the President of Yugoslavia, the President of Greece, the Vice-President of China, the Secretary General of the United Nations, and the leader of the Palestine Liberation Organisation, Yasser Arafat, took part in the funeral.

The entire India and the entire world bid farewell to Indira Gandhi with heavy heart. She had not died a meaningless death, she had faced death bravely and had given glory to both her life and her death.

Indira Gandhi was cremated with full state honours. The three Chiefs of Staff of the three wings of the defence forces led the procession carrying the dead body. Besides the three Chiefs of Staff who carried her bier, the first Field Marshal of India, Sam Maneckshaw, also lent his shoulder to her bier.

Indira Gandhi's dead body was kept on the funeral pyre, and amidst *Vedic mantras*, her son, Rajiv Gandhi, lit the pyre. The crowd of people who had gathered there were unable to control their emotions. The sound of sobs could be heard all around and the atmosphere resounded with the cries of "Long live Indira Gandhi."

Now, when Indira Gandhi was no more and India was bereft of its mother, and the world was bereft of one of its sensible people, then her memory became even stronger. The pain of losing her became sharper, more unbearable. In such emotional moments, many incidents about her were recalled.

People used to call her the Iron Lady. She was truly an Iron Lady. She was fearless in taking decisions and was a very disciplined lady. But, she was also very soft-hearted and very delicate and had all the qualities that characterise a woman. The sweet smile that played on her lips showed that although the high office of the Prime Minister that she was holding had forced her to become strict and disciplined, the softness of her heart still existed behind that hard facade.

Even today, many people remember that shy, innocent, delicate, and slim girl who later went on to become the Prime Minister of India. And there is no other equal of the determination and courage that she demonstrated as the Prime Minister of India.

Lakhs of Indian people admired her. People listened with attention to whatever she said and tried to follow that.

In this context, an anecdote by Najma Heptullah is very touching. Najma is the granddaughter of Abul Kalam Azad and she has very close relations with the Nehru family. After Azad's death, Najma stayed with her mother for some months in Teen Murti Bhavan. At that time, Pandit Jawaharlal Nehru was the Prime Minister of India and Indira Gandhi used to look after her father and used to greet the guests and look after them. Najma formed a close relationship with Indira at that time. This relationship continued till the end. Afterwards, when Najma went to live in Mumbai, Indira Gandhi used to meet her there also regularly. After Indira Gandhi became the Prime Minister, whenever she went to Mumbai, she would meet Najma every time.

Once, when Indira Gandhi went to Mumbai, she went to the market with Najma and other friends. Their car stopped at the Church Gate area. A few people went to the market. Indira Gandhi and Najma remained in the car. Standing near the car, at the side of the road was a small boy in tattered clothes. He was holding one or two packets of *agarbattis* in his hands. With eyes full of wonderment and fear he went near the car and pointed towards Indira Gandhi and asked Najma – "This is Indira Gandhi?"

Najma replied – "Yes."

The child looked at Indira Gandhi with wide eyes. There was a strange kind of a glow on his face and wonderment in his eyes. He said to Indira Gandhi – "I am not a beggar. I am not asking for alms from you. I sell these *'agarbattis'* to make my living. Will you buy my *agarbattis*?"

Needless to say that Indira Gandhi was extremely moved to hear the little boy's talk and was filled with pride.

This was the effect of Indira Gandhi's principles and ideals on the common people. She wanted to make India self-sufficient. If even little children of India are so full of self-respect, then it will not take India long to become self-sufficient.

She was never afraid of death. She had said in her last tour in Orissa that even if she had to sacrifice her life for her country, she would not be afraid.

So, this was the persona of Indira Gandhi and the way of her thinking, working, living, and dying.

How did she have so many good qualities? From where did she learn this unique way of living and this unique way of dying?

Why was she murdered? Who were those people who benefited by her murder? What was their motive? Was it a very big international conspiracy? Should any particular community be held guilty of her murder?

These were some questions which had no answers. Everyone was searching for the answers to these questions.

16

AFTER HER UNTIMELY DEATH

Getting caught up in religious intolerance, sometimes misguided people take such steps which are against the basic tenets of all religions. Does any religion give the teaching of hatred, enmity, and bloodshed? Religion always joins people and teaches them to love. How can we say that two people belonging to a particular religion murdered her? Can anyone say that they followed the teachings of their religion or they acted for their religion? No, no one can say this. These were misguided people who did not know the true meaning of religion. Such people are just symbols of a narrow mentality, they do not belong to any religion. Instead, they break the basic principles of religion by their acts.

Indira Gandhi was killed by two of her own bodyguards. The excuse they gave was that she had sullied the purity of the Golden Temple by sending the army there. The question here arises – does any religion become pure by doing something like this?

The dream of a united India always remained in Indira Gandhi's eyes, and her mind always thought of ways to maintain the unity and integrity of the country. She gave up her life for this high goal, in the end.

We don't think that Indira Gandhi would have any regrets about her death. Even though our eyes became wet with tears on her death, yet we all realise that she gave her life to protect a great principle.

The truth is that Indira Gandhi lived for the country and died for the country.

By Indira Gandhi's death, the entire nation was shocked and filled with grief. Not only the entire nation, but also the entire world.

She was not only the Prime Minister and a dear leader of India, but she was respected in the whole world and was a ray of hope for the entire humanity. Everyone knew that she was one of the sensible voices in world politics. Her efforts for world peace were praised throughout the world. That is why when in the year 1984, nominations of the candidates for the Nobel Prize were announced, Indira Gandhi's name was also included as a candidate for the Nobel Peace Prize.

Everyone loved her. The citizens of all countries loved her. Everyone felt shocked and saddened by Indira Gandhi's sudden death. Her assassination had a strong reaction in India.

Indira Gandhi had died on 31 October 1984 at 1, Safadrjung Road in the morning by the bullets of her bodyguards. When she was taken to the hospital, she had died by then. Despite this, the doctors made an unsuccessful attempt to revive her – because it was a part of their duty.

The official news of the death of the Prime Minister was given at 6 o'clock in the evening, but by afternoon, the news of her death had spread throughout the country and the world.

Whatever happened in India as a reaction to Indira Gandhi's death was most unfortunate.

On hearing the news of Indira Gandhi's assassination, in New Delhi, the anger of the people burst in the form of violence. Violent incidents took place in many parts of the country in which many innocent people were killed. Curfew was imposed in 30 cities in various states. The army was called in nine cities including Delhi. In Delhi, Patna, Kanpur, and Dehradun, shoot-at-sight orders were given. Extensive violence took place in many cities–Kolkata, Bhopal, Agra, Raipur, Jabalpur, Indore, Madhya Pradesh, and Rajasthan. Minor incidents took place at three or four places in Himachal Pradesh.

In contrast to other states, the situation remained calm in Punjab, Haryana, Chandigarh, Mahrashtra, and Gujarat. The army did a flag march in the sensitive areas.

Property worth crores of rupees was destroyed in many parts of the country due to looting, arson, and violence. The violent mobs burnt thousands of motor vehicles in different parts of the country. In Delhi alone, the violent mobs burnt about 2,000 vehicles.

Delhi

In Delhi, orders were given to shoot at sight any person indulging in violence or looting. Curfew was imposed in many areas and the army was stationed at many places. About 50 people were killed in the extensive violence, arson, and breakage that took place.

Madhya Pradesh

At least eight people were killed in the violence that took place in the different cities of Madhya Pradesh. Curfew was imposed in 12 cities of the state. The violent mobs burnt many shops and houses and indulged in looting.

In Bhopal, curfew was imposed till 3rd November. The army was called to maintain law and order in Jabalpur, Indore, and Sagar. The police fired many rounds to disperse the violent mobs. Curfew was imposed in Gwalior, Jabalpur, Indore etc. Approximately 500 people were jailed in the state as a precautionary measure.

Rajasthan

In Bharatpur city, there were some blasts, which were executed by a few Sikhs. Official sources said that no one was killed in the blasts. The blasts were very mild.

In Ajmer, five Sikh youths sitting in a taxi raised slogans in support of Bhindrawale. At one place, the youths got down from the car and waved their naked swords in the air. On seeing the police, these youths ran away.

In many villages of district Jaipur, the violent mobs set fire to the houses of many Sikhs. In Jaipur and Kota, some Sikhs were beaten up by the mobs.

Bihar

After some incidents of arson and looting in Bihar, curfew was imposed in Patna, Daltonganj, Ranchi, and Hazaribagh. The army did a flag march to prevent the violence from escalating in many parts of Bihar. The army was called out in Patna, Ranchi, Bokaro, and Dhanbad.

In the violence that followed more than 5,000 shops were looted. The police were given orders to shoot at sight in Patna. In Patna, the police fired bullets at three places, but there was no news of anyone being injured in this firing.

In all the cities of Bihar, prohibitory orders were issued and gathering of more than five people at one place and carrying of weapons were prohibited.

West Bengal

In different parts of West Bengal, five people were killed in the violence and due to police firing, and many people were injured.

Curfew was imposed in four areas of Kolkata, Vardhman and Asansol.

The army was put in charge of maintaining law and order in four areas of Kolkata. In Asansol, Vardhman, and Raniganj coalmine area, seeing the deteriorating situation, the army was put on alert.

Despite the presence of the army and armed police, incidents of arson and violence took place in four places in Kolkata. In two places, the religious places of a particular religion were burnt. In Maniktala Tirhati market, some shops were burnt.

Himachal Pradesh

The army was put on alert after some violent incidents and incidents of arson in Himachal Pradesh. In the Mandi district and in some other places, prohibitory orders were issued under Section 144.

In Joginder Nagar of Mandi district, a truck and some shops were burnt. An attempt was made to burn a religious place.

Everyone condemned the violent incidents that took place in Delhi and in other parts of India.

These violent incidents went on for only two or three days, but due to these incidents many people of one religion had to lose their lives or property. It is impossible in any way to compensate those people who lost a family member or property in this violence.

The government suppressed these violent riots with a heavy hand. But, the crack that formed in the relations between the Sikhs and the Hindus, took many years to seal.

But, the traditional and historic brotherhood and goodwill that existed between the Hindus and Sikhs also came forward during these violent incidents. Many Sikhs themselves say that on many occasions, the Hindus protected them and gave them shelter in their homes. The truth is that this brotherhood between the Hindus and the Sikhs is never going to end. The atmosphere of suspicion and mistrust that had formed was removed very soon when the people of the two religions met and interacted together.

When the violence was at its peak, the new Prime Minister was not quiet. On 1st November, Prime Minister Rajiv Gandhi had given clear and strict orders to the administration and the state governments that the violent incidents should be controlled at any cost and as soon as possible. The army was called out to control the violence at Delhi, Kanpur, Jabalpur, and Kolkata. The governments of all states were told that they could call in the army to help the police, wherever they felt that this was necessary.

The Central Home Secretary, Mr. Manmohan Krishna Bali, acted very calmly and wisely in the serious situation and requested the people not to believe the false rumours that were floating around.

The result of all these efforts was that the violence was suppressed within two to three days. An announcement was made that the affected people would be given monetary help. The property that was looted was restored to their owners.

On one side, violence was raging in many parts of the country, and on the other side, there was a very emotional atmosphere at Teen Murti Bhavan where Indira Gandhi's dead body was kept in state.

The ideals that Indira Gandhi strived for during her entire life, and in the end, she gave up her life for those ideals. To pay our true tributes to her, let us take the pledge that we will strive to maintain the unity and integrity of the country. Let us pledge that we will show religious tolerance, that we will keep alive unity and brotherhood, and that we will prove that the citizens of India are one and will always remain one. This will be our true tribute to Mrs. Indira Gandhi.

17

INDIRA GANDHI HAD SAID...

English

Today, if we are adopting English, then our intention is not that it should become the national language, that it should replace Hindi, Tamil, Bangla, or the language of any other state. This can never happen, and nobody wants this to happen also. But, we think that not knowing a foreign language will definitely weaken our position in the international arena and will impede our progress.

–From a speech in the Lok Sabha on the occasion of passing a Bill on Official Language (Amendment) (12 December 1967)

International friendship

I will work wholeheartedly for international friendship and peace, so that the people of the world are able to live a life free of fear and terror, so that all the people are equal and are independent.

–In a message to the nation (26 January 1966)

Good

Only that thing is good which benefits everyone equally.

–In a speech in Belgrade (8 June 1983)

Past and present

No country can exist only on the basis of its glorious past. To be successful in life, every person should try to develop his or her abilities continuously and should try to contribute in the development of the nation, without thinking about which religion or caste he belongs to.

–In a speech on the occasion of the seventh All India Muslim Educational Conference (New Delhi, 30 March, 1984)

About herself

My relations with animals started with my contact with snakes, because my maternal uncle was not only a very keen botanist, but he also had a special attachment to snakes. When I was about six years old, I used to go to stay at my maternal grandmother's house in Delhi. Whatever I opened, a snake used to pop out of it – whether it was a box of cigarettes, a drawer, or a bathroom pipe– although my grandmother did not like all this.

–On the occasion of the Mumbai Natural History Society centenary celebrations (Mumbai, 15 September, 1983)

My roots go very deep into the Indian culture because my entire education and upbringing focused a lot on the Indian culture. I belong to a family that was fully committed to the good of the nation and the people. My upbringing was also done in such a way that I grew up to think of myself as a citizen of the world. So, I do not see much difference in the various cultures of the world. There are differences in the various cultures, but one can also see many similarities in them. So, I do not like a thing only because it is Indian or dislike something simply because it is non-Indian. I like some things which are Indian and some things which are non-Indian.

–In an interview with Mr. Jean Pageau of the French National Radio (New Delhi, 12 February 1971)

I have enough sense to understand what my people are saying. If you want to live with peace and harmony, then I advise that you should first maintain law and order yourself, before expecting other people to maintain law and order.

–In a speech at the Ahmedabad Mill Owners' Association (24 January 1970)

Violence and lawlessness

No one benefits by lawlessness and violence, except those who want to harm the unity and integrity of the country.

–In a broadcast on All India Radio and Doordarshan (2 June 1984)

Rich and poor

It is the nature of the rich to say that the poor people are careless and lazy.

–In the inaugural speech at the first conference of the Asian Forum of Parliamentarians on Population and Development (New Delhi, 17 February 1984)

Failure

Any nation that vows to achieve progress and works collectively to achieve this goal can never be unsuccessful.

–In a debate in the Lok Sabha on a no-confidence motion (7 November 1966)

Non-violence

Non-violence is not a symbol of cowardice or surrender. Instead, when a person who decides to do a task is unarmed, then he needs more determination, discipline, and courage.

–In a speech at Belgrade (8 June 1983)

Independence

The meaning of independence is not only to have one's own government, but its true meaning is that we should be able to take decisions ourselves. These decisions may be wrong, but they should be our decisions, they should be the decisions of India.

–In a speech at the Ahmedabad Mill Owners' Association (24 January 1970)

If we have achieved independence, we should not rest peacefully that we have now achieved independence. We have to struggle always to maintain it. We have to protect this flame of independence from every storm, from every gust of wind, we have to save it with our hard work.

–From the ramparts of the Red Fort (15 August 1984)

The meaning of self-sufficiency is not that we remain aloof from the other people and other ideologies. The meaning of self-sufficiency is that we should adopt the tried and tested knowledge and mould whatever has happened outside according to the needs of our country.

–In a speech at the Science Policy Foundation (London, 26 March 1982)

As a nation, we should definitely encourage our ancient morality. We should continue in our efforts to make the weaker sections and other people self-sufficient.

–In a speech at a Chief Ministers' Conference (4 April 1983)

The secret of the strength of any nation is what it can do itself, not what it can borrow from others.

–In the foreword of the Fourth Five-Year Plan (18 July 1970)

Hospitals

A good hospital is like a big tree, which gives the shade of security; like churches and temples used to provide in the Middle Age.

–A.I.I.M.S (New Delhi, 23 March 1968)

Habits

The habits that are ingrained in us since many generations force us to remain in a limited area, and make us shirk from any kind of change.

–In a speech on the occasion of the release of the books of Swami Ranganathan (Delhi, 4 June 1971)

Modern history

Modern history is not the history of the royal dynasties; instead it is the history of progress. We should walk on the path of progress, but should not forget our ancient civilisation. But, besides this, we should also give an explanation of the teachings of our ancient civilisation in the modern context, so that the people of the present age understand the true meaning of our ancient civilisation.

–In a speech at the National Unity Council (20 June 1968)

Modernity

The meaning of modernity is not that we should copy the other countries. The meaning of modernity is that if something good has happened in other countries, whether it is in science and technology or something else, we should learn from that. But, we also have to generate new ideas and have to take forward what we have learnt from outside. Now what happens is that if we get any idea from outside, we follow that blindly. This is a work which does not happen by any government order. Our youth have to generate this feeling within them that they have to lift the country and the people upwards.

–On the occasion of the foundation stone laying ceremony of the new Yamuna Bridge in Delhi (29 August 1983)

Hope and faith

We should remember that only one thing is important in this world – hope and faith, no matter how low you may have fallen, how poor you may be, or how broken you may be.

–In a debate on a no-confidence motion (4 August 1966)

Waiting

Instead of waiting for others, we should make the first move ourselves. For this, we will have to sacrifice some small things like personal safety and comfort and will have to inculcate moral courage in ourselves.

–In a speech at a youth conference in Panchmarhi (11 June 1966)

Responsibility

Except totally selfish people, everyone feels responsible for someone or the other – it may be towards one's family, towards one's village, towards one's country, or towards humanity, which is the truest type of responsibility that one can feel.

–On being given a honorary doctorate degree in Fiji (26 December 1981)

Struggle for achievement

Anything worthwhile is never got easily. If you get anything easily and cheaply, then very soon you start feeling that something is lacking in that thing. Everything that is great in life – whether it is independence, equality, or brotherhood, is achieved by struggle, sweat, tears, and blood.

–In a convocation ceremony at Vishwabharati, Shantiniketan (2 February 1971)

Whatever progress takes place in the country, in whichever direction it takes place occurs only if there is unity, peace, a good economic situation, and political stability in the country.

–In a speech from the ramparts of the Red Fort (15 August 1968)

There are people belonging to different castes and different religions in India. There are people who speak different languages, people who live in different states. We want a bridge to be present amongst these people–a bridge, which is not visible. What should be visible is friendship – the feeling of brotherhood. We have to construct the bridges of love and cooperation.

–On the occasion of the foundation stone laying ceremony of the new Yamuna Bridge in Delhi (29 August 1983)

Art and entertainment

To stay alive, a human being does not only need food, he

needs art and entertainment also – personally and socially. He needs it for expressing himself, for expressing the different aspects of his personality, and for fulfilment. By laying the foundation of cultural give and take and goodwill, he can take his other tasks forward.

–In a dinner hosted on the occasion of a meeting of the Indian Chamber of Commerce in America (New York, 2 August 1982)

Kautilya

The book on political economics *'Kautilya ka Arthshastra'* (*Kautilya's Economics*) is a gift of ancient Bihar to not only India, but also the whole world.

–In a speech on the occasion of the silver jubilee function of the A.N. Sinha Institute of Social Studies (Patna, January 1984)

Poets

No society can remain alive without poets. In India and in all other countries, the poems and the national anthems have played an important role in the struggle for independence. The history of our independence struggle is full of the stories of the poets who inspired the people with their poems. In our *'prabhat pheris'*, in the processions that we used to take out all day long, and in our meetings, the inspiring songs and poems of the poets used to remove the tiredness from our feet and the worry from our minds. We used to sing these songs in jail to keep our hope and courage alive. These inspirational words used to bounce off the walls of the jail, to prove to the people that nobody could dampen our enthusiasm, and no one could turn us away from our goal. Even today, these words resound in my ears.

–On the occasion of the releasing ceremony of Dr. Bacchan's collection of poems (New Delhi, 8 August 1983)

Dedication to work

Every citizen should have a desire in himself to contribute to the progress of the country. We all like to work in good working conditions, but we should do our work without bothering about good working conditions. I want our students to say, "Whatever happens, I will remain alive for my country and do such work by which my country progresses and by which I am able to leave my mark on my country." We achieved independence by this type of determination, and even ordinary men and women became brave due to such determination. Now we have to take a new vow to take our country forward on the path of progress.

–In a speech at the Indian Agricultural Research Institute (10 February 1968)

Agriculture

The meaning of achieving self-sufficiency in agriculture is to not only become successful in giving food to our growing population, but we should also try to produce enough for export. We should try to increase food production as soon as possible, so that our country becomes self-sufficient in this. We should find ways to infuse enthusiasm into our villagers and to channelise their entire energy into constructive works. We have to infuse a new life into the progress of the villages. We have to try to increase the income of the farm workers.

–In a message to the nation (26 January 1966)

Poverty

Poverty is a very fearsome situation that brings about a feeling of hopelessness in the people and weakens the country. So, our first task is to remove poverty from the country. To achieve this goal, we have to remove social and economic inequality from the country.

–From the ramparts of the Red Fort (15 August 1971)

Struggle against poverty

There is one war which is going on along our borders, and there is another equally important war which is being fought in our country. This is the war with poverty and backwardness. We will not be able to fight this battle till we adopt new ideas and till we remove superstitiousness from our midst. We will not be able to fight this battle till we decide that no matter how many sacrifices we have to make, no matter how many hardships we have to face, we will do what needs to be done and that everyone will take responsibility for his actions. This is the responsibility of every single person and now the time has come when we cannot shirk from that responsibility. We cannot remain mute spectators to what is going on in the country. We should be soldiers of the country, not mute spectators.

–From the ramparts of the Red Fort (15 August 1966)

Non-alignment

In today's fast-changing world, peaceful coexistence is more important than it ever was. Despite the breaking-up of the old groups and the emergence of new centres of power, non-alignment is still important today. Non-alignment softens the tension that occurs due to the formation of new kinds of alignments. It simplifies the process of separating oneself from power groups following different types of ideologies. It gives more strength to independent nations against outside pressure. The philosophy of non-alignment is based on the principle of friendliness with everyone.

–In a broadcast from All India Radio (7 July 1966)

To students

To those people who are studying, I would like to say that life is not an exam similar to the exam which you give in schools and colleges. Life is an exam that goes on continuously; it is a challenge that one has to face continuously. Almost everyday, you have to take some decision in life. If you like something, you have to take a courageous stand to declare to the world that you like something. You need mental courage for a right decision, and moral and physical courage so that you are able to walk on the path you have chosen.

–In a speech at a convocation ceremony in Vishwabharati, Shantiniketan (17 December 1983)

Democracy

True democracy cannot function without tolerance and goodwill towards everyone: Tolerance and goodwill not only towards those whom we like, but like my father used to say "also towards those whom you don't like."

–On the occasion of the birth centenary celebrations of Gopalkrishna Gokhale (New Delhi, 9 May 1966)

Population control

As a mother and a Prime Minister, I am fully aware of the rights of a child on love, care, and the basic necessities of life. I am also fully aware of the problems that the mothers have to bear to look after their children. If we are in favour of limiting the size of the family, then it is due to the fact that we care about the health of the mothers and because we love our children. We want our children to live in a world that gives them the full opportunity to develop their personality. We want our children to live in a world whose foundations are laid on the stones of peace, prosperity, and human values. For this, we need to have peace in the country, we need to have peace in the family, and we need to have peace in the world.

–In the inaugural speech at the first conference of the Asian Forum of Parliamentarians on Population and Development (New Delhi, 17 February 1984)

Growth in population

The youth should come forward to participate in the campaign to control population and to encourage development. Awareness should be inculcated in them about the consequences of a growing population, through schools and colleges and other methods of informal education. They should be aware of the consequences of a growing population, which can affect theirs and the nation's future adversely. Programmes to impart awareness on population control should be implemented at various stages so that at the time of marriage, the youth are aware of their responsibilities towards the future generation and the society. At places where people gather together on the occasion of festivals etc., there is a very good opportunity to give information to the youth about the importance of these programmes for population control.

–In the inaugural speech at the first conference of the Asian Forum of Parliamentarians on Population and Development (New Delhi, 17 February 1984)

Awakening

If the country progresses, then we will also progress. Even if we don't want to progress, then also we will progress if the country progresses. If the country weakens, then everyone will weaken, no matter how rich or influential he is. He will become weaker compared to the rest of the world.

–On the occasion of the foundation stone laying ceremony of the new Yamuna Bridge in Delhi (29 August 1983)

Science and technology

Science and technology are the foundation stones on which the progress and future of the human beings are built. It is the work of the educationists to turn them in the right direction and to use them in the right way. Education is necessary for the well-being and welfare of human beings. Wellbeing means progress, and welfare means development. Progress is a material thing, and development is a spiritual thing. The addition of both of these will, in my view, make education more meaningful. The educationists should think about this and should try to put it into practice.

–On the occasion of the silver jubilee function of the Gorakhpur University (11 November 1983)

Three great teachers

I have had the honour of being close to many great people, who were famous not only in India but the entire world. The roots of our cultural traditions are very deep. In spite of this, we have always thought about the future. Amongst my great teachers, the first was Gurudev Tagore in whose university, Shantiniketan, I spent one year. Another of my teachers was the Father of the Nation, Mahatma Gandhi. In his prayer meetings, discussions used to be held on various topics. Some of these meetings seemed very ordinary at first look, but Gandhiji never considered anything or any person to be small.

My father was one of the many friends of Gandhiji. He was also one of my teachers. His language was very simple, whether it was on political, economic, scientific or foreign policies or whether it was for illiterate villagers.

–On being given a honorary doctorate in Fiji (26 September 1981)

Riots

Most of the riots are incited by a handful of people or sometimes even one single person. But, due to the atmosphere of mistrust and misunderstandings, or due to narrow attachment to the caste, religion, or language, the personal enmities turn into a collective enmity.

–At the National Unity Council (12 November 1980)

Dictatorship

Dictatorship can exist only for a short duration. Due to this, the progress becomes faster for some time. History has proven that such shortcuts solve some problems, but give rise to many more, much more complex problems.

–In an interview published in 'Revista de Occidente' of Madrid, Spain (19 March 1968)

Showmanship

The false showmanship of one's wealth and property gives rise to many kinds of social tensions.

–In a speech at the Indian Merchants of Chamber (Mumbai, 25 October 1967)

Unity of the country

No matter which party or ideology we belong to, we have to remain united for the security, unity and integrity of the country. Today, we should have only one slogan, and that is – 'We should be one, we should be united, and we should move forward.'

–From the ramparts of the Red Fort (15 August 1971)

Policies of the country

The policies of any country are formulated keeping in mind its national interest. Before formulating any national policy it is necessary to think what the traditions and heritage of that country are and what the needs of the citizens of that country are. The foreign policy is a reflection of the internal activities of a country. Is it not possible for us to achieve our national goals by integrating them with collective benefits and acting in cooperation with others, so that we collectively benefit from them? I think that this can happen and this should happen. Our foreign policy of peace and cooperation, which is based on the principles of peaceful coexistence and non-alignment, strives towards these goals.

–In a speech at the 57th Conference of the Interparliamentary Union (New Delhi, 31 October 1969)

Rules and regulations

No government can function without rules and regulations. But, these rules and regulations should not be inflexible. They should change according to the changing circumstances. We cannot consider such a situation to be satisfactory in which it is easier to bring about an amendment in the Constitution instead of changing the so-called 'fundamental rules' or the 'civil services rules.'

–In a speech at the annual meeting of the Indian Institute of Public Administration (New Delhi, 22 October 1971)

For the weaker sections of the society

India has come out of darkness. It is probably the first time in the last three or four years that we are sitting in the light of the Sun, and this light has lighted up our entire country. Although there is light in many areas, many houses, and in many cities, how can we forget that there are still many houses in which there is darkness? How can we forget those farmers on whose land there is no irrigation? How can we forget crores of our '*harijan*' brothers and sisters, or our brothers and sisters belonging to the backward castes, or those who live in the mountains, or those who live in the jungles, and our '*adivasi*' brothers and sisters? In their houses, the light of independent India does not shine as brightly as we had promised them it would shine after independence.

–From the ramparts of the Red Fort (15 August 1966)

Family planning

The meaning of family planning is not only to limit the population or to slow down the rate of population increase. The meaning of family planning is to make a better family, to make such a family in which the parents are able to pay full attention to the needs of their children.

–At the annual meeting of the Indian Council for Child Welfare (3 April 1967)

Hard work

Any society, whether it is a capitalist or a communist society, has been able to progress only when its citizens have worked hard, have faced hardships at every step and have never become demoralised. When the citizens have taken risks, made mistakes, and learnt lessons from those mistakes, only then have they been able to climb the peak of success.

–At a convocation ceremony in Vishwabharati, Shantiniketan (15 February 1969)

Police

The police also needs the cooperation of the people. If the police are always perceived as an enemy of the people, then they will have difficulty in behaving in a way which is compassionate and friendly.

–In the Lok Sabha, replying to a debate on the expenditure of the Home Ministry (24 June 1971)

Trees

Trees are amongst the most faithful friends of human beings. Whichever country wants to improve its future should take good care of its forests.

–In a speech at the Forestry Education Centenary Function in the Forest Research Institute, Dehradun (19 December 1981)

Savings

The message that we have to spread in all corners of the country is to save as much as possible, and to keep the saved money in banks.

–In a speech at the Bankers' Club (Chennai, 5 October 1969)

Curbing infantile diseases

When the parents are fully assured of the health and safety of their two children, then they would desire to limit the size of their family. Therefore, the importance of curbing and treating infantile diseases has grown. There is a need to pay special attention to nutrition and the treatment of diseases.

–In the inaugural speech at the first conference of the Asian Forum of Parliamentarians on Population and Development (New Delhi, 17 February 1984)

Intelligence

In philosophy and in science, those people search for the truth who are more intelligent.

–In the inaugural speech at the 71st conference of the Indian Science Congress (Ranchi, 3 January 1984)

Future

The burden of future is heavier than that of the present.

–On the occasion of the silver jubilee function of Gorakhpur University (11 November 1983)

India's unity

Beware against such talk which encourages mistrust and weakens the country. We have to remain united for the security of our country. We have to remain united for the unity and integrity of the country. We have to work together to make our country stronger and more developed. The future of every person, every section of the society, and every state depends on how strong the nation is. Only a powerful and stable India can become the ambassador of peace and friendship in the world.

–In a message to the nation (15 January 1984)

India's ideals

We are forgetting the ancient ideals of India. We talk about religion and tradition, but we forget what is at the root of religion and tradition – goodness, charity, consideration for others, helping others, and most important, to maintain an atmosphere of peace. If we forget these ideals, then how will we progress?

–From the ramparts of the Red Fort (15 August 1984)

Indian women

The women of our country did not have to struggle against the men for their rights, as the women in the western countries had to struggle for their right to vote. The women of our country fought shoulder to shoulder with the men for independence and for their fundamental rights. When we were insulted, when we were beaten up, when we were put in jails, or when we were hanged, then nobody used to show preferential treatment to us due to being women. We have contributed equally in the struggle for independence. So, shouldn't we have equal rights on the fruit of that independence? The equality of men and women is an integral part of our Constitution.

–In an interview published in 'Revista de Occidente' of Madrid, Spain (19 March 1968)

Fate

I don't leave everything to fate. Fate helps only those who pull it close to themselves by the determination of their character.

It is not something which comes in flapping its wings, through the window. You have to work hard to make your fate.

–In reply to a question at a press conference (New Delhi, 31 December 1971)

Indian education system

I am among those people who criticise the Indian education system and believe that there is room for much improvement in this. But, still I believe that despite all these shortcomings, this system has produced many scientists and great people, and this process is still continuing.

–In the inaugural speech at the 71st conference of the Indian Science Congress (Ranchi, 3 January 1984)

Indian culture

Since the ancient times, the attitude of the Indian culture has been a positive one. It has not been one of separatism, but one of joining and bringing together.

–In a speech at the 57th Conference of the Interparliamentary Union (New Delhi, 13 October 1969)

Writers

Whether writers come into politics or whether they do not come into politics, they cannot disregard the challenges and difficulties of life. They cannot disregard the joys and sorrows of the people; otherwise what type of literature will they create? Shouldn't the writers try to enrich human life through their poems and essays, through their plays and books?

–In a speech at the fourth Afro-Asian Writers' Conference (New Delhi, 17 November 1970)

Young men and women

The young men and women of our country should get more opportunities. They should also be made to understand that what they give to their country today, the country will give back to them tomorrow. The country expects them to have a high morale, high ambitions, and accomplish big tasks.

–In a debate in the Lok Sabha (1 March 1966)

Youth

Our youth should try to start their own work. More and more people should try to start their own businesses–such businesses which they think are safe and reliable.

–In a speech at the National Cooperative Council of Young Entrepreneurs (Mumbai, 25 October 1969)

Science and technology

Without understanding history, culture, and the hopes and aspirations of the people, science cannot work for the welfare of the people. Therefore, it is necessary that material science and technology work together with human and social sciences. It is necessary that all their efforts be directed towards moral values and social goals.

–At the annual conference of the Indian Science Congress in Varanasi (3 January 1968)

Culture

Culture is not something which one can force on someone, it is something that should arise from within the human beings.

–In the inaugural speech which was read out at the 58th annual conference of the Indian Science Congress in Bangalore (3 January 1971)

Truth

The truth has to be discovered afresh by every generation. In any age, the people of that time need to discover the truth themselves, no one learns from mistakes of the past.

–In the inaugural speech at the Committee of Educationists and Youth Leaders (New Delhi, 16 January 1970)

World peace

International cooperation is an integral component of India's efforts to achieve a progressive economy and a democratic society. This is the reason why after achieving independence, we have accepted that world peace and world cooperation are integral to India's national interests.

–In a speech at the Royal Institute of International Relations (London, 29 October 1971)

Goodwill

Mahatma Gandhi had once said and my father repeated it time and again that we have to work hard to wipe the tears from every single person's eyes in India. It is truly a very difficult task to accomplish and it is not possible for any nation to accomplish this task.

–In a speech given at a dinner hosted by President Johnson (Washington, 26 March 1966)

Cleanliness

It is the duty of every citizen to keep his country neat and clean. It is very surprising that in a country where religion has given so much importance to cleanliness – like giving importance to cleanliness in eating, bathing, washing hands and feet – in such a country we have to appeal to people to try to keep their cities and villages clean!

–In a speech to the legislators of Andhra Pradesh (Hyderabad, 26 July 1972)

Internationalism

All human beings are one, but their backgrounds and their nationalities are different. They are at different levels of progress and may have different political views. This difference is necessary for the existence of the world. The attempts to force the people to adopt one ideology have not only been unsuccessful, but have also proved to be dangerous to peace. All our policies are based on this principle. Although some people might consider peaceful co-existence to be a useless thing, yet this is the foundation of international relations. Its roots in the reality of the present times have become strong and it is the basis for the existence of all human beings.

–In a speech given at a dinner party for the Soviet Prime Minister, Mr. Kosygen (New Delhi, 25 January 1968)

International disputes

We don't believe in using power to solve international disputes. But, if someone tries to suppress us, then we will definitely answer back. India is not greedy for anybody's land. We don't want to interfere in anybody's internal affairs and neither do we want to influence any nation forcibly by our ideas and our policies. We believe in the independence of all countries. This policy of ours of living together with peace and harmony is not new. This is based on our traditions. We have got this faith from Buddha, Gandhi, and Nehru. We are busy in making a new society in India based on democracy and socialism. We believe that only by giving equal opportunities and rights to all sections of the society and ending inequality will the citizens get full benefits.

–In a speech at a royal dinner given by the King of Nepal (Kathmandu, 4 October 1966)

Superstitiousness

If we are not able to obtain victory over superstitiousness, then we have to use this superstitiousness to our advantage. Behind many of the superstitions are religious principles. It is easier to say that it is God's will instead of saying that it is my own will. If you do something on God's name or attach the name of some small god or goddess to what you do, then it does not matter if it benefits some people in the end.

–In a speech at a laboratory of the Council of Industrial and Scientific Research (New Delhi, 3 July 1982)

Officials

Any such official, who does not believe in secularism, cannot tackle the problem of communalism. We should all be committed to the progress of the country and should have a feeling of commitment towards the welfare of our countrymen.

–In a speech on the golden jubilee conference of the Institution of Engineers (Kolkata, 14 June 1972)

Struggle for independence

During our long struggle for independence, we did not think that after achieving independence, our goal would be achieved. We understood that independence was that key by which the doors to opportunity and progress would be opened.

–In a speech at a huge meeting in Kuala Lumpur (31 May 1968)

Discipline

If we want to make the children disciplined, then first we will have to make the entire society disciplined.

–At the annual meeting of the Indian Council for Child Welfare (New Delhi, 3 April 1967)

Without discipline, we cannot take the full benefit of education. Any programme that is intended for the children can also not be completed without discipline.

–At the annual meeting of the Indian Council for Child Welfare (New Delhi, 3 April 1967)

Disunity

Whenever we have been disunited, we have had to pay the economic and political price for that. Whenever narrowness came into our ideology and whenever we fought amongst ourselves, our independence was snatched away from us by foreign powers.

–In the inaugural speech at the All India National Unity Conference (New Delhi, 12 January 1984)

Undivided society

We should not only think about how the society should be, we should also think about how the people living in this society should be. It is certain that we do not want a society that is divided into two parts: One part which controls the thinking of others, and the other part which is controlled by others. We want such thinking individuals in our society who are able to work independently. We want such individuals who are themselves interesting and take an interest in others also. We want such individuals who are inspired by sympathy and empathy towards others.

–In a speech at the United Nations' Conference on the Human Environment (Stockholm, 14 June 1972)

Incompatibility

Whenever there is incompatibility between the mind and the heart, we feel uneasy – like science without spirituality, knowledge without conscience, intellectualism without understanding. All these should be turned towards good thoughts, and such works should be done whose goal is good of all.

–In a speech on the occasion of silver jubilee function of the A.N. Sinha Institute of Social Studies (Patna, January 1984)

Desire for independence

Throughout history, people have been murdered, people have been wounded, they have been suppressed; but nobody has been able to suppress the feeling of humanity, the feeling of independence, and human glory. We have seen its evidence in India and every such country, which has fought the war of independence. This emotion of human beings has helped them progress and helped them attain new heights. India can definitely not support anyone who suppresses such human glory and the desire for independence. We also don't believe that peace can be established by oppression. You can postpone the coming of independence, but you cannot stop it forever.

–In a speech at a function organised by the Indian Students' Association of Washington (Washington, 5 November 1971)

Revolution

Due to continuous revolutions, our limited resources can become even lesser and in this way our development programmes can take longer to complete. These revolutions, which are constantly going on in our country or the threats of such revolutions, affect our development programmes very adversely.

–In an appeal to the people of Assam (19 October 1969)

Soul

Human beings think themselves to be very great. The magnificence and majesty of the mountains and their peaceful high peaks enable us to see our activities and ourselves in the right perspective. How small and insignificant we are, and despite our powers of destruction and creation, how helpless we are in the hugeness of the universe! But, still we have a special thing and that is our invincible spirit. It is on the basis of this invincible spirit that men and women become capable of changing the impossible into possible.

–In a speech at the silver jubilee function of the Indian Mountaineering Association (27 August 1983)

Economic independence

Without economic independence, political independence is incomplete. The other countries put pressure on the newly-created and developing countries till the time they are not able to achieve economic independence. But, it is necessary to oppose such pressurising. The chasm between the poor and the rich countries is growing wider. Due to this, new tensions have arisen. It is the duty of international diplomacy to remove these tensions.

–In a speech at the Indo-Soviet Friendship Association (14 July 1966)

History

Whatever we do, we cannot disregard history. If we do so, then it will leave us behind and move forwards. If we keep sticking to those inferences, which have been derived from those institutions, which have lost their meaning, then also this danger arises. If we keep repeating the old mistakes again and again, we move more and more farther away from reality.

–In the inaugural speech at the 44th annual conference of the Federation of Indian Chambers of Commerce and Industry (New Delhi, 10 April 1971)

Production and talent

The measuring yardstick of success is production and talent. Its true test is not only to earn profits, although that is also important. But, its true test is – what is the standard of quality of the finished products, how much benefit do people get from them.

–Addressing the chief functionaries of the public sector undertakings (New Delhi, 5 April 1983)

Industry

Industry is perhaps one of our nation's most urgent necessities. Industrialisation will help us in the fields of agriculture, science, and even in removing the communal and other types of tensions that plague our society. Industrialisation will help smoothen those tensions which manifest themselves from time to time and endanger our unity, put hurdles in the path of our progress, and sometimes endanger our very existence.

–In a speech in the National Cooperative Council of Young Entrepreneurs (Mumbai, 25 October 1969)

Colonialism

The obstacles that have been put in the path of progress of the new nations, these can be called a new type of colonialism. Economic, technological, and communication methods have been used to put obstacles in the path of new nations. We raise our voice against this type of colonialism. That is why we lay emphasis on a new economic system, new communication system, and the need to recognise our culture. These walls in the path of progress cannot be removed, but they can definitely be crossed.

–In a speech at the 38th session of the General Assembly of the United Nations (New York, 28 September 1983)

Neglected

Any society is judged by how it treats its most neglected class of people. In India also, we have to face this challenge because in India, like other developing countries, the number of neglected people is very large. This section includes not only the sick and the handicapped people, but also a large number of such ordinary people who can be considered as handicapped due to poverty and economic backwardness.

–In a speech at the 12th International Leprosy Conference (New Delhi, 20 February 1984)

Unity

Today, the independence of the nation is in danger. If we are not strong, then we cannot be successful in anything. Whether it is religious goodwill or equal opportunities for the minorities – all these are parts of unity and goodwill.

–In a speech at the 18th conference of the Presidents of the Social Welfare Boards of the States (14 July 1983)

The meaning of unity can never be mental bondage, because India's prosperity is in its great diversity. Diversity should be allowed to flourish in its own way.

–In the inaugural speech at the Committee of Educationists and Youth Leaders (New Delhi, 16 January 1970)

The problem of unity should also be seen in its social and economic perspective. To end the tensions, it is necessary to have a fast rate of growth and progress. Undoubtedly, this includes helping all weaker sections, those who are economically and socially weaker, and those who are downtrodden.

–In the inaugural speech at a meeting of the National Unity Council (New Delhi, 21 January 1984)

It is our duty to maintain unity, and we cannot maintain unity by fights in roads and lanes. It is not the duty of the government, government officials, and political parties only; but of the ordinary citizens also that conflicts and disputes should not be solved on the streets, but should be taken to those institutions, which have been constituted for this task. These matters should be discussed and decided there. We have to decide if we have faith in the Parliament and the parliamentary method or hooliganism and rioting.

–In a debate in the Lok Sabha (23 February 1968)

Unity is not a question of only religion, language, or area, but it is an economic question also.

–In a speech at the Chief Ministers' Conference (4 April 1983)

No nation can neglect its security. It cannot make this assumption that because it is strong, its neighbouring countries will not attack it. It has to remain alert always. It always has to take care that it does not lag behind in the field of technology. We should also not think that just because we are independent and have a Constitution, social unity will come itself. It also has to be guarded like the borders of the country. Armies are there for the protection of the borders, but the entire burden of social unity lies on the citizens.

–Inaugural speech at the All India National Unity Conference (New Delhi, 12 January 1984)

Unity and independence

We have already suffered a lot due to internal conflicts. Now, we have to come together and decide that we will not let anybody endanger our unity and independence.

–In a speech at the Ghalib Award Ceremony (New Delhi, 6 July 1984)

Law

Law is a special profession, which needs qualities of deep study and introspection. And more than that, it needs a commitment to justice and the desire to protect the innocent and to punish the guilty. The commitment to law and justice is not limited to only the lawyers, it is found in all human beings. It is also necessary for all human beings to have this quality because without law and order, a harmonious life is not possible.

–In a speech at the third International Appellate Judges' Conference and Commonwealth Chief Justices' Conference (New Delhi, 5 March 1984)

Strictness

I don't want to say that you should act with strictness. I don't believe in strictness, but I definitely believe that there are many times when we cannot succeed without determination. When basic questions are raised, when fundamental values and ideals are hurt, when other people are used to weaken us – at that time every citizen should fulfil this responsibility. Every citizen should think that the future of its future generations is in danger. He should speak against this in India and outside.

–In the inaugural speech at the All India National Unity Conference (New Delhi, 12 January 1984)

Danger

We can be separate in politics. But, we are united by our brotherhood, our tolerance, our friendship, and our goodwill. Due to this unity, we can face the biggest dangers. Today, the dark cloud of violence and hatred has cast its shadow again. Our unity is being hurt again. People are being misled and they are being turned away from the path of progress. Every Indian should realise what dangers the nation is facing because that danger is a danger to him also.

–In a speech at the Ghalib Award Ceremony (New Delhi, 6 July 1984)

Contemplation

Contemplation and creation, both of these should be born out of an enquiring analysis of the social situation. This is the same spirit of enquiry which gave birth to the leaders of revolution in France. It gave birth to Lenin and Gorky in Russia, to Tagore, Gandhi, and Nehru in India.

–In a speech at the fourth Afro-Asian Writers' Conference (New Delhi, 17 November 1970)

Rural India

Rural India is thirsty for science and technology. Rural India has an infinite amount of everything that is needed by scientists – whether it is human talent or those raw materials, which are obtained from the plants and trees. Our scientists have to do something to fulfil these requirements.

–In a speech at the golden jubilee function of the Indian National Science Academy (New Delhi, 16 January 1984)

Challenges

If there are no challenges and no hard work, then there can be no success. In India, we do not want a life of relaxation. We don't want our path to be strewn with flowers. We want challenges, by which we can prove that we can face them and be victorious over them.

–In reply to a question at a press conference (New Delhi, 31 December 1971)

Life

Life is ever changing. All aspects of life are inextricably intertwined with each other. Every action in life has a reaction, which can be felt on all the aspects of life. The boundaries between all specialist areas of life are slowly becoming invisible. Therefore, to make their work more effective and to provide for the future, people should keep a wider goal in front of their eyes – which may require them to extend the scope of their professions to encompass a wider canvas.

–In the inaugural speech at the 44th annual meeting of the Institution of Engineers (India) (New Delhi, 21 May 1971)

The country: a family

Every country is a huge family. Those countries whose income and resources are limited should have such an economy where the necessary requirements are not neglected and wastage is stopped. The resources should be divided equally and priorities should be decided. The arrangements for education and other social necessities should be in such a way that the poor and other weaker sections of the society derive special benefit from it. There should be a balance between agriculture and industry, technology and culture, public and private sector undertakings, and economic progress and social justice. Every section of the society should be inspired to take part in constructive tasks.

–In a speech at a dinner given by the Indian Chamber of Commerce in America (New York, 2 August 1982)

Religion

We can be honest towards our religion only when we recognise the right of other people to be honest towards their religions. We should not forget that the limit of any right is only to the extent where the rights of other people start.

–In the inaugural speech at the All India National Unity Conference (New Delhi, 12 January 1984)

Blind copying

No country can progress by blindly copying another country. If we want to chalk out new paths of progress, then we have to pay the price for these also because you don't get anything free in life – neither anything small is free, nor anything big is free.

–In a speech at the Indian Merchants' Chamber (Mumbai, 25 October 1969)

Spirituality

The meaning of spirituality is the equality of the soul, the strengthening of the conscience of human beings, and the spreading of realisation. It is that ability which makes a human being peaceful in situations of chaos and fully aware and alive in moments of peace. It gives the ability to human beings to keep themselves separate from time and circumstances and to retain equanimity in moments of happiness and sorrow. Farsightedness and mercy are the signs of true spirituality.

–In a speech at the meeting of the United Nations' Conference on the Human Environment (Stockholm, 14 June 1972)

Secularism

The meaning of the word 'secular' is not that we are anti-religion. Instead, the meaning of this word is that in the eyes of the government, there is equal respect for all the religions of the world. It means that every citizen, no matter which religion he may belong to, has equal rights in the eyes of the law. The government itself does not have any religion. It cannot have any religion. If the government has a religion, then those people who don't follow that religion, will not feel that they have equal rights.

–In a speech at a function organised by the Indian Students' Association of Washington (Washington, 5 November 1971)

Instability

Where there is instability, indecision, and insecurity; economic progress is not possible there. In such an atmosphere, any attempt to bring about economic equality will not be successful. In such an atmosphere, each time the law and order is broken, the poor people will suffer more as compared to the rich people.

–In a speech at the Indian Merchants' Chamber (Mumbai, 25 October 1969)

Soldiers of peace

Today, we will take a pledge that the soldiers of our war of independence and those who are soldiers in this new war of progress will inculcate the same madness within themselves, which was found in the soldiers of the war of independence. Today, we shall create that revolution, which does not let us sit, which whispers continuously in our ears, hearts, and minds – Come, awaken, Mother India is waiting for you. Mother India is calling you, this country needs you.

–From the ramparts of the Red Fort (15 August 1966)

Official mindset

This official mindset is also responsible for putting obstacles in the path of progress. This symbol of colonialism still has a very strong influence on everybody. This officialdom was born during the days of our slavery.

–At a convocation ceremony of Roorkee University (18 November 1967)

Self-sufficiency

The meaning of self-sufficiency is not to separate oneself from others. This means to interact with others on an equal footing and to forge better and more productive economic relations with them. In political and economic matters, true self-sufficiency can be established on the foundations of complete independence.

–In a speech at a dinner given in honour of the then Prime Minister of Nepal, Mr. Kirtinidhi Bisht (New Delhi, 18 April 1972)

Self-acceptance

It is true that we have made mistakes. When someone has to do so many things at the same time and on such a large scale, in such circumstances, which the others have never faced, then it is not possible that all the things are done without any mistake. We are able to realise our mistakes much more than is pointed out by our bitter critics, and we are trying with a true heart to remove those shortcomings.

–In a speech at the 57th Conference of the Interparliamentary Union (New Delhi, 31 October 1969)

Ideals

Ideals are those goals which you strive for. It is not something which you can achieve immediately. An ideal is inspirational in itself because the desires of the people are not stable. As soon as they achieve something, they desire something more, and this is correct also.

–In a debate in the Rajya Sabha on the Fourth Five-Year Plan (13 August 1970)

Modern technology and developing countries

To get more technical know-how, the developing countries have to pay an economic and political price. And it is often seen that only old technology is sold. Basic and complete technical know-how is not sold. In the area of nuclear sciences, the atomic powers who are continuously increasing their nuclear capabilities, have created the hoax of nuclear proliferation and have tried to divert our attention. In this area, many types of restrictions are attached to any kind of cooperation and they are given the name of security.

–In the inaugural speech at the 71st conference of the Indian Science Congress (Ranchi, 3 January 1984)

Industry

Whether it is a communal attitude due to which we consider someone to be big only on the basis of his religion, or consider someone to be more patriotic than others, or deprive someone of the right to stay in his desired part of the country or join the desired profession – all these are attitudes which weaken the nation. Till a cordial atmosphere is not there, till there is no unity, until the desire to work together is there, till then no industry can flourish and no progress can be possible.

–In a speech at the National Cooperative Council of Young Entrepreneurs (Mumbai, 25 October 1969)

Industrial areas

Our industries can progress only when there are people to

show us new directions and to take us in those new directions. I believe that once Mahatma Gandhi had said that we cannot create history by repeating the experiences of others. We have to be ready to create new paths for ourselves. We may make mistakes, but we can learn lessons from our mistakes, and in this way move towards new achievements.

–In a speech at the National Cooperative Council of Young Entrepreneurs (Mumbai, 25 October 1969)

Farmers

The farmers of India are our backbone. The country cannot remain alive without them and cannot move forward on the path of self-sufficiency without them.

–From the ramparts of the Red Fort (15 August 1980)

Oppositions to wrong traditions

It is necessary to remove poverty, but it is equally important to make this country a modern and wise country. By this, I don't mean that we should forsake all our values and traditions. We should take from the past all that is permanent and that which has not changed with time. But, we have to fight against all that is narrow-minded, which encourages superstition, which has lost its meaning in today's progressive society. To believe that some people are small only due to their caste or religion does not hold any meaning in the present times. Our society is only weakened by such beliefs.

–In a speech to the legislators of Andhra Pradesh (Hyderabad, 26 July 1972)

Working together

If some person is not able to do big things then he should aim at doing well the small things that he can do. If we have a common goal, then our efforts should also be common. Come, let us do our work unitedly, so that we are able to achieve our goal easily.

–In the inaugural speech at the 44th annual meeting of the Federation of Indian Chambers of Commerce and Industry (New Delhi, 10 April 1971)

Guru Gobind Singh

It was his belief that temples and mosques are one. He believed that human beings divide themselves by fighting in the name of food, dress, traditions, and religion. He used to say, "It is my goal that the entire humanity live together as brothers and sisters. Then, how can I love one brother and hate another brother?" He was the incarnation of forgiveness. When even someone who had betrayed him would come and ask for forgiveness, he would say– "We don't dwell upon things that have happened in the past."

–In a radio broadcast on the occasion of the third birth centenary celebrations of Guru Gobind Singh Ji (18 January 1967)

Peoples' awareness

Our people are not fully aware about ancient traditions, our unique struggle for independence, and our present process of progress and achievement. They are also not aware of the dangers that our country faces.

–In a speech at the silver jubilee function of the A.N. Sinha Institute of Social Studies (Patna, January 1984)

People power

The future of the nation depends on our education system and the ability of the youth. The biggest treasure of any nation is its people. A nation is constructed by new ideas and talent, and the key to both is education.

–In a broadcast from All India Radio (19 October 1966)

Our most valuable resource is people power. But, this is a statement which needs to be repeated again because we have been neglecting our people power. We know that if we do not utilise it to the fullest, it can become a curse for us, which can give rise to frustration and disappointments and result in violence. But, if this people power is used to encourage economic progress, it will become a very big boon and it will create a strong foundation for the progress of the nation.

–In a speech at a Conference of the Chief Secretaries of the States (New Delhi, 12 April 1971)

Facing the enemy

Whether it is the government or the people of India, all of them know fully well that they will get nothing from fights and conflicts. With cooperation and friendship, everyone will be able to solve their problems and will be able to help each other. Those who are our enemies, those who want to put pressure on us, those who want to move us, and want to stop us from becoming strong, we will face them – not with weapons, not with fights, but with our strength, our stability, our unity, and with our ideals.

–From the ramparts of the Red Fort (15 August 1980)

The feeling of patriotism

The challenge that is facing us at this time can only be overcome when the Indian professional class, scientists and technologists, actually the entire country, works with discipline and a commitment to the supreme feeling of patriotism.

–Inaugural speech at the 43rd annual conference of the Federation of Indian Chambers of Commerce and Industry (14 March 1970)

Women

Women have a very big role to play in creating the future. What effect have they on their children and their house, how they inculcate good habits – the society will change only by this and it will progress only by this. Good health depends on good habits. If mothers and children know about these, then it will save them from a lot of illnesses.

–In a speech at a women's meeting (Kavaratti, 10 October 1969)

Neighbouring countries

I want to assure the people of the neighbouring countries that the people of our country want to have friendly relations with them. We don't want conflicts. We know that everyone cannot have the same opinion about everything, there will always be conflicting opinions. But, wherever we can come to a common decision, there we should try to help each other, there we should walk with each other. If we cooperate with each other, if we help each other, then a lot of our expenses will also come down and our strength will increase. But, if people threaten us, then we are ready for that also.

–From the ramparts of the Red Fort (15 August 1980)

We don't want to interfere. We don't want to put obstacles in the unity of any other country. It is not in our interest also to interfere in any other country's internal affairs. We want that our neighbouring countries should remain stable, should remain strong, and should have friendly relations with us. So, we extended the hand of friendship and we said – If we can hold talks, if we can arrive at a mutually acceptable decision, then that will be helpful for you also and we will also be saved from difficulty.

–From the ramparts of the Red Fort (15 August 1984)

Caste

Can there be any greater false propaganda than this that one caste is superior to another caste? It is indeed unfortunate that there are still some people who don't judge people by their values and intelligence, but by their colour and body structure.

–On the occasion of Mrs. Martin Luther King being given the Jawaharlal Nehru Prize (New Delhi, 24 January 1969)

Bureaucracy

It is not necessary that only those who are in bureaucracy are bureaucrats. Wherever you might be, you can be a bureaucrat, because bureaucracy is really the name of an attitude. I don't mean to say that all bureaucrats behave in a bureaucratic way. But, bureaucracy is a type of mentality, which we should all guard ourselves against. Wherever we might be, we should make the attempt to not look at the face of the government for everything. We should take inspiration from the people around us, from society, and we should generate the desire to work from within ourselves.

–At the 18th Conference of the Presidents of the Social Welfare Boards of the States (4 July 1983)

Nuclear non-proliferation treaty

We are independent people, so we become suspicious of anything which can be harmful to our independence. Why do outsiders dictate such terms which increase the international inequality and dependence? Nuclear non-proliferation treaty is basically discriminatory. We have refused to sign this. Those nations which do no shirk from using nuclear science for military purposes, what right do they have to stop other nations from using it for peaceful purposes even?

–In a speech at the Science Policy Foundation (London, 26 March 1982)

Environment protection

There is a need to have a very large-scale campaign to teach our people the basic principles of environment conservation. These lessons should be imparted along with school lessons. The people should be taught that we have to plant trees and have to protect them, and have to look after the animals and the birds.

–Inaugural speech at the 10th General Assembly of the International Union for Conservation of Nature and Natural Resources (New Delhi, 24 November 1969)

Technology

Technology should be transferred in such a way that any nation can adopt it according to its social and economic situation while simultaneously encouraging its own scientific research. When there is transfer of technology by private mediums and multinational companies, then the goal of that transfer is to earn profits. Some areas of the economy of the developing countries are joined with international markets and modern technology, and most areas remains backward due to being connected with the traditional methods of production. This type of technology transfer does not result in the development of the entire economy and this type of technology transfer is meaningless for most of the people. The technology transfer, which takes place in private institutions and public sector enterprises, should be made more meaningful.

–In a speech at Belgrade (8 June 1983)

Outside interference

Every country has its own personality, its own specialities, its own beliefs, and its own political system. While ourselves believing in non-alignment, we respect the right of every nation to choose its own path and to form its own government without any outside interference. Besides this, we also know that it is our duty to solve whatever disputes there might be with discussion and goodwill.

–In a speech at the Conference of the Foreign Ministers of the South Asian Countries (New Delhi, 1 August 1983)

Indian philosophy

Compared to the west, our philosophy is flexible. Examples can be found in our ancient mythological tales of almost all situations and modern ideologies. Why don't we use our ancient wealth of knowledge to solve our present problems?

–In a speech at the 70th annual conference of the Indian Science Congress (Tirupati, 3 January 1983)

Language

Language is a means of transfer of knowledge. Due to political interference, its importance lessens. Similarly, to drag religion into politics is to make religion narrow.

–At the third World Hindi Conference in New Delhi (28 October 1983)

18

APPENDIX

(1) Jawaharlal Nehru

(14 November 1889 — 27 May 1964)

Bharat Ratna Pandit Jawaharlal Nehru was born on 14th November 1889 in Allahabad in a rich Brahmin family of Kashmir. At the age of 16 years, he went to England. There, he studied in the famous Harrow School and Cambridge. In 1912, he returned to India and practised law for some time. In 1919, he became a member of the Indian National Congress. Very soon, he became a leading soldier of the national movement. Due to his taking part in the Indian struggle for independence, the British government imprisoned him nine times from 1921 to 1945. After independence, he became the first Prime Minister of India and throughout his life (till 27th May 1964), he remained on this post. During his term as Prime Minister, India became a republic on 26th January 1950 and its Constitution came into being. He implemented the Five-Year Plan for the development of the nation. He started the Non-Aligned Movement. He was the founder of this movement and one of its foremost leaders. Today India is moving ahead on the path of progress that Nehru showed to independent India.

Jawaharlal Nehru was a good writer also. During his imprisonment, he wrote many books, including his autobiography. Some of his famous books are – *'Glimpses of World History'*, *'The Discovery of India'*, *'An Autobiography'* etc.

(2) Rajiv Gandhi
(20th August 1944 – 21st May 1991)

Rajiv Gandhi was born on 20th August 1944. His father's name was Feroze Gandhi and mother's name was Indira Gandhi. His maternal grandfather was the first Prime Minister of India, Jawaharlal Nehru. Two years after Rajiv's birth, his father was transferred to Lucknow. He was transferred there as the Managing Director of the *'National Herald'* newspaper. The family came to live in Lucknow. When Rajiv was six years old, Indira Gandhi came to Delhi. Rajiv was also with her. His father stayed in Lucknow to look after the management of the *National Herald* newspaper.

Feroze Gandhi had participated actively in the struggle for independence. After independence, he was elected twice to the Lok Sabha from Rae Bareli– in 1952 and then in 1957. His campaign against corruption is remembered even today.

For his primary education, Rajiv was admitted in the Welham School of Dehradun. In 1955, he started his education in the prestigious Doon School. On 8 September 1960, when he was 16 years of age, his father died.

In 1962, Rajiv Gandhi went to London. There he studied at the Trinity College and Imperial College. In London, he met Sonia, who later became his wife.

Rajiv was interested in flying planes since the beginning. In England, he used to learn how to fly planes in his spare time. After returning to India in 1967, he was trained as a pilot in the Indian Airlines in Hyderabad and on 5th May 1968, he formally joined Indian Airlines as a pilot.

He did not like politics, but after the death of his younger brother, Sanjay Gandhi, he had to come into politics. He joined politics in 1980. In 1981, he won the Lok Sabha elections from Amethi. On 17th August 1981, Rajiv took the oath of office as a member of the Lok Sabha. On 11 March 1982, he was made the General Secretary of the All India Congress Committee. During this time, he looked after the work of the Congress Seva Dal and the Youth Congress.

On 31st October 1984, Indira Gandhi was assassinated. That

same evening, a grieving Rajiv was made the Prime Minister of India. In the elections held in the same year, the Congress Party, under his leadership, won 401 out of 508 seats.

During his term as the Prime Minister, many improvements were made at the administrative, economic, and technical levels. Amendments were made in the Constitution for judicial and electoral reforms. Panchayati Raj was implemented. The age of voting was reduced from 21 years to 18 years. In the field of education, he established the Indira Gandhi National Open University, which is today benefiting lakhs of students the world over. He paid special attention to international relations.

He wanted to establish India as a big power by the beginning of the 21st century. Unfortunately, the Congress was removed from power in the general elections held in December 1989. V.P. Singh became the Prime Minister. But, this government did not run for very long. Rajiv Gandhi was again being seen as the next Prime Minister of India, but on 21 May 1991, in a public meeting in Sriperumbudur (Tamil Nadu), a human bomb took his life and this bright star of the Indian political horizon faded forever.

(3) Sonia Gandhi
(9th December 1946)

Mrs. Sonia Gandhi was born on 9th December 1946 in a middle class Italian family. Her ancestral village is in Orbasano, about 12 miles from Turin in Italy. Her father's name is Stefano Maino. She is the second of the Maino couple's three daughters. Her elder sister's name is Anukama and younger sister's name is Nadia.

Mrs. Sonia Gandhi's initial education was in a Catholic school situated in Italy. Afterwards, she obtained a diploma from the Cambridge University of London in English language. For her family, Sonia was like a princess. She was okay in studies, but not very intelligent. Her father was highly influenced by the Russian language and culture. This is the reason why he gave his three daughters Russian names. Sonia learnt the Russian language from her father. She knows Spanish, English, and French languages also equally well.

Sonia inherited the maximum amount of her father's good

qualities of hard work and discipline. Sonia was very naughty when she was young and a very active little girl. She used to play football with the neighbourhood boys for hours or used to play hopscotch with them. Sometimes she used to get very violent. When she was young, once she hit one of her friends on the head with a thick dictionary. She was very ambitious when she was young and wanted to be a teacher, but her mother wanted her to take up a more paying job. Her mother and father used to quarrel often due to her father's strict disciplinarian nature, so Sonia became closer to her mother.

Sonia's name was attached to the famous Gandhi family of India in the year 1968. She met Indira Gandhi's son, Rajiv Gandhi, in 1965 when both of them were studying together at the famous Cambridge University of Britain. Both of them started liking each other. Then, they started meeting each other regularly. They dated each other for about three years and used to meet frequently at a Greek restaurant in the city. One day, Rajiv went to Sonia's ancestral village, Orbasano, and asked her father, Stefano, for Sonia's hand directly. Stefano was shocked. He said to Rajiv that if his love for Sonia was true, then he should stay away from Sonia for one year, and then he would make his decision. Both of them stayed separately for one year, but their love didn't lessen in fact it grew even more. Then, Stefano half-heartedly gave both of them the permission to marry. He was worried about how would Sonia, who had been born and raised in Italy, adjust to the Indian culture and traditions. This was the reason why he gave Sonia a return ticket. He believed that Sonia would not be able to stay in India for very long. But, Sonia never returned to Italy. On 13th January 1968, Sonia first set foot on the soil of India. On 25th January 1968, she was engaged and one month after that, on 25th February 1968, on the day of Basant Panchami, she was married to Rajiv Gandhi.

Rajiv and Sonia's wedding was very simple. In this marriage ceremony, which took place at 1, Safdarjung Road, Sonia had worn the same pink cotton saree which her mother-in-law, Indira Gandhi, had worn on her wedding day. The speciality of this saree was that the thread that was used to make this saree had been spun by Jawaharlal Nehru himself when he was in prison.

Sonia soon became close to everyone in the Gandhi family, especially Indira Gandhi. Both of them used to like each other very much. It was due to their close relation that the time passed easily and happily for them. Sonia was never interested in politics. She did not want Rajiv to come into politics. Once, she had even threatened Rajiv that she would divorce him if he joined politics. Although, in this context, Rajiv said that Sonia had said so because she was afraid of losing him.

The author of *'Indian Dynasty'* Tariq Ali has written at one place that Sonia Gandhi had once said to her friend that she would prefer to make her children beg on the streets rather than let Rajiv join politics. But, in the end, what Sonia was afraid of did happen. In 1980, after Sanjay Gandhi's death, Rajiv resigned from the Indian Airlines and joined politics. Ali writes that Rajiv had made this decision after talking about it for hours with Sonia. But, today after her husband's death, Sonia herself is playing an important role in politics.

Sonia joined active politics in the year 1998 and in a very short time she took the Congress Party, which was reduced to the sidelines, to the forefront.

(4) Rahul Gandhi

(19th June 1970)

Rahul Gandhi was born on 19th June 1970 in Delhi. At the time of his birth, his grandmother, Indira Gandhi, was the Prime Minister. Afterwards, his father, Rajiv Gandhi, became the Prime Minister. Later, his mother, Sonia Gandhi, sacrificed the post of the Prime Minister after almost reaching there. Rahul's great grandfather, Jawaharlal Nehru, was the first Prime Minister of the nation and remained in the post till his death.

Rahul Gandhi completed his education at Junior Modern School in Delhi, St. Columba's School, and St. Stephen's College. He was a good shooter. He won many national awards in shooting.

After completing his primary education, Rahul went to London. There, he did the Bank Secretaryship course in Harvard University and started working in London. In 1999, he returned to India and started helping his mother in the election campaign.

Rahul Gandhi is still unmarried, but it is said that he is close to a Venezuelan (in South America) girl called Joanita. Joanita works in a departmental store in Madrid and meets Rahul very often. Sonia's elder sister, Nadia, had introduced her to Rahul. During the new century celebrations, she had come to the Andaman Islands with Rahul as his guest. Some Congressmen who oppose Rahul's marriage to her believe that the addition of another foreigner to 10, Janpath (Sonia's official residence) will not be politically beneficial to the Congress. As far as Sonia is concerned, she is of the opinion that she has given her children (Rahul and Priyanka) the independence to take their own decisions.

The elections to the 14th Lok Sabha were held in 2004. Rahul also jumped into politics. He contested the elections from Amethi and was victorious from there.

(5) Priyanka Gandhi
(December 1971)

Priyanka was born in December 1971 in New Delhi. At the time of her birth, her grandmother, Indira Gandhi, was the Prime Minister of India. Before her, her great grandfather, Jawaharlal Nehru, was the Prime Minister of India. Afterwards, Priyanka's father, Rajiv Gandhi, became the Prime Minister of India.

Priyanka completed her education from Junior Modern School in New Delhi and then Jesus and Mary College. She married Robert Vadra on 18th January 1997. They have a son and a daughter.

Rahul and Priyanka are like the right and left hands of their mother, Sonia Gandhi. Due to their constant efforts, Sonia Gandhi joined active politics. Till 1994, both Rahul and Priyanka also did not have any interest in politics. Priyanka and Rahul got full love and affection of their grandmother, Indira Gandhi. Although, Sonia and Rajiv were strict parents, Indira used to protect the children from the scoldings of their parents. Due to security reasons, the education of Rahul and Priyanka had a lot of ups and downs.

19

GLIMPSES

On 12 June 1975, the Allahabad High Court declared Mrs. Indira Gandhi's election from Rae Bareli to be invalid. To protest against this decision and to demonstrate his political power, Sanjay organised a public meeting at the Boat Club in New Delhi. About one lakh people took part in this rally. To demonstrate the unity of his family, Sanjay asked all his family members to come to this rally. It was very painful for Rajiv and Sonia to go to this rally because they did not have any interest in politics. Sonia went to the meeting wearing a cotton khadi saree. She stood on the stage behind Indira Gandhi with Rajiv, Maneka, and Sanjay. Sonia had seen such a big crowd for the first time in her life. Her eyes were filled with wonder at how Indira Gandhi could mesmerise such a big crowd with her speeches.

****

Sometimes, big quarrels took place in Indira Gandhi's house also, especially during the emergency. One day, Maneka got angry with her husband, Sanjay Gandhi, due to something and she removed her wedding ring and threw it in front of Sanjay. Indira Ji got very angry with her daughter-in-law at this act of hers because that ring had the legacy to her mother, Kamala Nehru. Sonia picked up that ring and said that from then her daughter, Priyanka, would wear that ring. Even today, Priyanka wears that ring on her hand.

****

After being defeated in the elections of 1977, Indira Ji came with her family to live at 12, Willingdon Crescent. This house was comparatively smaller than the Prime Minister's residence. Here, Indira Ji and Sonia came closer. Maneka used to feel jealous as to why her mother-in-law liked her elder daughter-in-law more. There were no *ayahs* or servants there. Sonia used to look after both her children, Rahul and Priyanka, herself. She also cooked the lunch and dinner herself. Sonia used to buy the vegetables and other necessary household items from the nearby Khan Market herself. She started growing cauliflower and other vegetables in the back garden of her house so that the requirement for vegetables would be met from there.

****

Indira Gandhi had a premonition about her death. Probably, that is why she used to tell her grandson Rahul again and again that if something happened to her, he shouldn't cry. On that fateful day of 31 October 1984 when Indira Ji was assassinated, her granddaughter Priyanka had got ready to go to school. Suddenly, a wave of affection swept over Indira Ji and she embraced Priyanka. She reminded Rahul of her words. After a few moments only, Sonia heard the sound of bullets. She came running and saw that Indira Ji's body was soaked with blood. She laid Indira Ji's head on her lap. Indira Ji was rushed to the hospital. But, she could not be saved. Afterwards, the official announcement of her death was made. Sonia still gets upset when she thinks of that moment.

20

INDIRA GANDHI IN SONIA'S EYES

"My mother-in-law was very wise and she soon became very close to me. She let me do everything myself. She never put pressure on me to do anything, which she thought I would not like. I think, that this was a very good way of helping me integrate with the family, and slowly I became a part of the family. Slowly, I was able to do all that which, if she had forced me to do previously, I would not have been able to do then. For example, if we went to a wedding, she never told me – You have to wear a saree or you have to eat Indian food only. Slowly, I started liking Indian food and now I cannot live without it."

****

"She was a very determined woman with a strong willpower. But, she was very gentle and soft from inside, and very few people know this fact. If anyone became a little bit sad or angry, she would immediately come to know of it and would definitely do something for them. I remember that when I had got newly married, my mother had come here and had stayed with us for one month. When she was returning, it was definitely a sad moment for me. My mother-in-law realised this immediately and said to me – 'Sonia, I just want to tell you that we all love you very much.' And, I got a lot of strength on her just saying that."

****

"When there were any challenges in front of her, she would face them in the best possible way. If there was any pressure on her, she would arise from that also and give the best possible answer to that."

****

"When she lost the elections, she herself said that she had thought again about the decision to implement emergency first and then announce the elections. It is proved by this that she had thought again about her decision to implement the emergency."

****

"It seems to me that she accepted that her decision to impose emergency was wrong. But don't forget that as far as I have been able to understand her, she was very deeply democratic. I think that the circumstances forced her to take that decision, but she was never happy about the decision she took."